The
POWER
of One Accord

Second Edition

The
POWER
of One Accord

7 Spiritual Keys to Harness Synergy in the Boardroom

Second Edition
Revised and Expanded

Charline E. Manuel

A One Accord Strategies, Inc. publication

Charline E. Manuel

A One Accord Strategies, Inc. publication

Previously published as *The Power of One Accord: 7 Spiritual Keys to
Consensus Building for Spirit Led Boards*

ISBN-13: 978-0-9779937-0-3

Cover design: Kyle Stephan

*Dedicated to Unity Center of Miami
in gratitude for the opportunity to serve,
and to the boards of trustees for the lessons
we learned serving together.*

Also by Charline E. Manuel

Pray Up Your Life

Pray Up Your Life Self-Exploration Companion Workbook

The Metaphysics of Shoes

Do Puppies Pray?

Content

How good and pleasant it is when God's people live together in unity!

Psalm 133:1 (NIV)

Introduction to this Second Edition, 2018

This second edition of *The Power of One Accord* conveys a few updates designed to improve board engagement by strengthening relationships around the boardroom table. As presented in the first edition, governance does not have to be divisive nor antagonistic. Rather, this book is launched from the ideal that when boards function as a unified team and together champion the mission and vision, good governance can happen. Surely effective governance will have opportunities for the expression of a variety of opinions, points of view and different perspectives. This kind of dialogue is necessary and important to building toward the goal of one voice. Standing unified around the decisions made allows board members to authentically claim a power that comes with harmony focused in the same direction. With harmony around decisions made focused on advancing the mission and vision, good governance has a chance to impact the work of the organization and its purpose for being.

Some of the updates have come as a response to feedback from the many boards who decided to use the book as a study guide and ongoing reminder of the principles presented herein. To facilitate this idea a new section has been added at the end of each chapter titled Discussion Starters for Board Bonding. The questions highlight ideas from the chapter to stimulate respectful sharing of different perspectives and views around the boardroom table. These Discussion Starters provide the opportunity to build healthy dialogue into the board's culture.

Other minor changes appear as a result to editing corrections. There are also changes made for greater clarity.

Finally, the subtitle of the book has been changed to reflect a more focused commitment to the purpose of the book, *7 Spiritual Keys to Harness Synergy in the Boardroom.*

Discussion Starters for Board Bonding

Discussion Starters for Board Bonding is placed at the end of each chapter. It is series of questions designed to "start" conversations that can build rapport, trust and strengthen the ability to communicate purposefully and freely.

With this kind of dialogue among the board, we build a culture of shared understandings, growing mutual respect and the opportunity for friendly associations. Through improved and increased communication, the dialogues can generate ideas and fresh perspectives on issues facing the board. This time of connection can also be the inspiration to work toward the benefits and values that evolve from full input and the contribution from the skilled, talented, diverse group of people sitting at the boardroom table. This level of mind, thought, heart participation can very well be an important key to developing a highly functioning board.

You may consider scheduling these discussions as part of your ongoing board development exercises, setting aside some time between board meetings to discuss by phone or video chat, a luncheon for board bonding or simply by taking one discussion point per board meeting asking each board member to come prepared to share. Be creative and do what will work for your board. Enjoy the sharing!

INTRODUCTION
to the First Edition

After three years, I found myself staring into the day I had hoped I could avoid, dodge, pretend would not come. I could no longer go along with how the majority members of the board wanted to handle the affairs of our spiritual community. I was hesitant as it was the board that hired me. In the first eighteen months, the honeymoon was a glorious love fest of compliments and support. But living in the afterglow, my enthusiasm for serving in our ministry had been shaken. Amidst growing mistrust, and what felt-like a struggle for power, secrets came to light and cooperation became increasingly more difficult to achieve.

As time progressed, I prayed, visualized harmony being restored, and decided not to rock the boat; rather, I would keep the peace. When I woke up that morning with a knot in my stomach simply because it was the day of our monthly board meeting, I knew I was in trouble. The stress was affecting my body and that was my final signal that something had to change. I felt out of sync with my call to ministry as I was not prepared to handle the wide range of thoughts from doubting myself, doubting that I was in my right and perfect place, doubting the prayerful decisions I had made regarding the church. "Had I followed Spirit's guidance?" I searched my heart thoroughly before going to the meeting that night, but that did not prevent the eruption of anger and several "unkind" words being spoken on my part and the part of board members.

The months that followed were filled with deception, misrepresentations and division. Daily, I questioned my call to ministry. I went over my clear guidance to accept the invitation as minister to the church by the board that now seemed to despise me. I interrogated myself, *how could such a good thing turn out so poorly? How could the light of clear guidance fade into a fog of confusion and uncertainty?* My body continued to ache, mostly in my gut. This was not how I wanted ministry to be and I didn't know how to make it right, except to consider leaving.

Thank God I had the support of a group of ministers who surrounded me with prayer and who counseled me through many, many difficult days. The sleepless nights ended when a colleague told me to read 2 Chronicles 20:17. I found great comfort by resting in the promise of those words: "You will not have to fight this battle. Take up your positions; stand firm and see the deliverance the LORD will give you, Judah and Jerusalem. Do not be afraid; do not be discouraged. Go out to face them tomorrow, and the LORD will be with you,'" (2 Chronicles 20:17 NIV). Then I prayed something like *Dear God, restore to me the passion and joy I had for ministry with a vision to serve in a vibrant ministry.* In seconds, an inner response came from my gut, "Stay, you're already there." And, while my guidance revealed that I was to stay, I had surrendered all my "warring" so completely that I spoke with my then eleven-year-old son saying, "There is a big meeting tomorrow at the church that will determine if we will continue to stay here or if we will be moving."

"Moving? Where?" he asked with surprise in his voice. Thank God he had not been affected by the many months of what I had been going through in the church.

"I'm not certain, but either way, stay or go, we're going to be okay."

The morning of the meeting, I was so calm and peaceful that I can say to this day, I know what total surrender feels like. I had put out a call to Jesus that day asking that the Christ spirit enfold me with full trust in God. I can say I prayed "Thy will be done," and on that day I meant it with every fiber of my being.

The meeting was immediately after the Sunday service and the church was full. There were faces I hadn't seen in a while and I knew they were there to see or watch what was about to go down. It was a special meeting called as a result of a petition that members filed with the board, after hearing that they planned to fire me. The meeting turned out to be a face-off between me and four members of the board who had been actively campaigning with present and past members to relieve me of my duties.

I did not speak during the meeting. As four of the six board members spoke, mostly in anger, I listened with so much love for them that I knew the spirit of Jesus Christ was upon me. I felt "Father forgive them, heal their anger for they do not even know that I have totally surrendered the outcome of this meeting to Spirit and all I can feel for them is love."

The remaining two board members stood up to speak, they asked that I not be removed as the minister and led a prayer for divine order then opened the floor for comments. The overwhelming majority of those who stood up to speak that day asked that I not be released. People stood up to speak some I barely knew. Finally, the four angry board members stood up and gave the congregation an ultimatum saying, "We've been at this church for many years; we even held this church together before she arrived, we hired her, but if she stays we go." As they spoke I was amazed at how peaceful I felt. It seemed like those words would have felt like daggers pounding into me but all I felt was "a peace that passed all understanding." One by one people began to stand up "The minister stays," over and over again, until about eighty percent of the two hundred people present where standing.

The four, walked off the platform and headed toward the door. I stood up and followed behind them and said to each one before they walked out. "This is your church, you don't have to leave."

The main spokesperson said, "I'll never set foot in this church again."

"If you ever change your mind please know that you will always be welcome here," I responded.

As I write this some sixteen years later not one of them has set foot in the church again. I ran into two of them some years ago at a public function and they were friendly, we hugged, and I invited them to church, but to this day they have not returned.

xiv The Power of One Accord

The lessons from that experience left me with a new-found commitment. I became intentional in my decision to make my relationship with subsequent boards a priority.

I would make sure all newcomers to our board would be willing to be in relationship with me and fellow board members. The good thing about starting over with a mostly new board was that while our wounds were fresh, everyone wanted to restore peace and harmony and they were willing to do whatever it took. Sixteen years later we are still doing many of the things we instituted back then: (1) We take an annual retreat that is mandatory for all board members; (2) we pray together regularly; (3) before our Saturday morning board meetings, we have breakfast together and check in with each other (this makes for longer board meetings, but for us it is worth it); (4) we have an annual board appreciation lunch or dinner where board members can invite partners/spouses; and (5) the 4T Prosperity Class is a requirement for board service and tithing is a must.

We're far from a perfect community, but the relationships on our board always remind me of Acts 2:46: "And they, continuing daily with one accord in the temple, and breaking bread from house to house, did eat their meat with gladness and singleness of heart." I have discovered that Spirit can accomplish far greater things through a unified dynamic team who recognizes their value to the fulfillment of a great mission and promise.

—Charline Manuel 2014

FOREWORD

I have written this book promoting and encouraging the idea of harmony within the board of trustees of a spiritual community. The harmony I speak of is: between the spiritual leader / minister and the members of the board, and between board members. The value of harmony on the leadership level of a spiritual community is obviously important, but the methods to achieve it are not always so obvious. I believe it is worth making the pursuit of harmony a conscious priority for those who serve in a leadership capacity.

In *The Power of One Accord*, I offer the idea of synergy as an outgrowth of harmony. Harmony is not presented as compromise or a weakness in leadership strategy, but as a method of operation arrived at through the application of the seven main principles offered here in seven chapters. With a focus toward activating the power of "one accord," agreement becomes a powerful magnet to attract and demonstrate the great blessings our ministries deserve.

Besides having one extremely difficult experience with my board some sixteen years prior to writing this book, I have seen and known of similar difficulties for many of my colleagues. Some of those experiences served as the beginning of the end of the minister's tenure in their ministry, resulted in divisiveness in the church, or became the instigating factor to the minister leaving ministry altogether. Of course, many worked through the challenges and healing happened, but not without great effort and a commitment to do the required work—inner and outer to achieve some sense of harmony.

Having gone through what was then my most difficult time in ministry and survived it as a learning experience, my heart goes out to those who are actively seeking harmony at the boardroom table. I pray you will find something of value in these pages.

Again, this book is written from my personal experience as a spiritual leader in the same church for nearly twenty years. They are the beliefs and attitudes I have developed toward board service and the relationships around the boardroom table. If any part of my experiences can be of assistance in your spiritual community I will have done as Spirit has guided me to do in this endeavor.

The Banquet Approach

Of course, every ministry is different, and every spiritual leader is different. Some of what you will read in these seven chapters simply may not fit your ministry style, culture, size, belief or interest. But as I was writing this book, I thought *I wish I had read this material nineteen years ago, had it in my reference library or simply had parts of it to discuss with board members over the years.* So if there is one thing, one idea, one concept herein that can support the establishment, restoration, maintenance, reconciliation, or movement toward greater harmony, it may be worth it in terms of wear and tear on the minds and hearts of the members around the boardroom table and the overall ministry.

My suggestion is to use what appeals to your ministry and leave the rest. If there is value, adopt pieces of these ideas in stages and tailor to meet your ministry's unique needs and desires. Or, simply consider using the material as conversation starters during board retreats where there is time to discuss subject areas of interest or concern. Open communication on ministry issues can be a healthy method in strengthening the soundness of relationships around the boardroom table.

Let Not Language be a Barrier

A single word can have many different connotations and evoke a variety of emotions and reactions. So, for that reason I say do not let my use of certain words become a barrier to the idea being presented. For example, I use God and Spirit interchangeably. I also use minister and spiritual leader interchangeably.

When I speak of "the board," I generally include the spiritual leader or minister since in most cases that person is a member of the board.

However, certain issues are specific to the minister/spiritual leader, and certain issues are specific to the members on the board absent of the minister/spiritual leader. In these instances, I make a distinction between the two.

I write from the generic "we" meaning those who serve on boards in general. When I speak of specific instances from my experience, I use "in our ministry 'we.'"

And of course, the word "church" brings up a variety of emotions. So here I refer to church, center, spiritual community, ministry, faith community as one in the same.

Finally, I speak of harmony "around the boardroom table" referring to the relationship of the board members when they convene as leaders and decision makers for the ministry. The same harmony they share as they fulfill their role as board of trustees, do we expect to exist beyond the boardroom. The harmony we strive for shall be reflected in the attitude and consciousness within the individuals who find themselves seated at the table of leadership, and that reflection shall prove itself by their experience and example in and out of the boardroom.

A Note on Babies and Bath Water

I have used several scriptural references that are attributed to the apostle Paul. Let me just say that prior to my challenge with my board many years ago, I simply was not attracted to much of the bible beyond the Gospel of John. I just did not delve into the ideas in the Epistles and Letters knowing that the writers spoke to and from a culture that I chose not to relate to. I had Jesus and we seemed to be doing just fine. Plus reading some of the statements attributed to Paul pushed a few of my personal buttons such as: "Let your women keep silent in the churches, for they are not permitted to speak; but *they are* to be submissive, as the law also says. And if they want to learn something, let them ask their own husbands at home; for it is shameful for women to speak in church," (1 Corinthians 14:34-35 NIV).

But when I found myself hungry to heal the error thoughts that were obviously part of my consciousness regarding minister and board relationships, I was willing to reconsider my way of thinking. So, I went to my bible and finally surrendered to the prompting to give Paul another try. I wanted to know what biblical ideals I could use for working with my board in a loving and harmonious way. And, after all who better than Paul would have a unique perspective on church administration that I could at least glean a few ideas from.

I realized that regarding my resistance to *all* of what Paul taught, I had missed *some* of what could actually be very helpful. I had thrown the baby out with the bath water.

As I opened my mind to search for what I could do to make my relationship with the board one that I could live with, I found so much more. I discovered ideas on how I could actually enjoy a healthy, respectful, productive relationship that has become one of my most cherished aspects of ministry. I discovered amidst what I saw as Paul's dogmatic language and his narrow perspectives on women and marriage that if I could understand and accept our differences of time, space, culture and consciousness, I would find the spirit in the words attributed to a man who no doubt had a deep love and passion for Jesus Christ.

Paul's passion stemmed from a transformative experience where he saw the light of truth that changed his life—I had found commonality between Paul and myself. With a changed mind, my heart opened, and I could hear his words differently.

While I still don't agree with *all* the words attributed to Brother Paul, I know that amidst those words there are some really sound spiritual principles that have and can support good church administration. However, I do believe that if Paul were around today he might look back on some of his former perspectives and the words associated with those beliefs and say something like, "When I was a child, I spake as a child, I understood as a child, I thought as a child: but when I became a man, I put away childish things," (1 Corinthians 13:11).

After all, isn't that what we all strive to do? As we grow in consciousness we change our minds. In the words of Charles Fillmore co-founder of Unity, "I reserve the right to change my mind." I was able to write this book because I changed my mind, an act that has once again, blessed my life, and by extension, those around me.

—Charline E. Manuel

Second only to the relationship we have with Spirit, the relationship between the spiritual leader and the board of trustees, and the relationship among members of the board is the most important relationship in a ministry. Christ centered harmony at the boardroom table is the blessing we all want — but it takes conscious, consistent effort to achieve and maintain.

Chapter One

Answering the Call to Serve

PURPOSE

"I therefore, the prisoner in the Lord, beg you to lead a life worthy of the calling to which you have been called, with all humility and gentleness, with patience, bearing with one another in love, making every effort to maintain the unity of the Spirit in the bond of peace. There is one body and one Spirit, just as you were called to the one hope of your calling, one Lord, one faith, one baptism, one God and Father of all, who is above all and through all and in all."

--Ephesians 4:1-6 (NRSV)

If Paul had been living a life focused on his own personal will, his message to the Ephesian church leaders might have been "Hey guys pray that I get out of here soon, prison is a *bleep!*" In Ephesians 4, Paul refers to himself as "the prisoner in the Lord." Yes, he's locked up, but Paul's attitude toward his imprisonment is not just about his outer experience. While his body is incarcerated his mind is free to live the life that Jesus Christ has revealed as the way, the truth and the life. The moments that changed his state of consciousness remain fresh in his

1

mind and heart. He cannot escape the effects of the experience that led him to know Jesus Christ, although at that time his name was Saul.

> "Meanwhile Saul, still breathing threats and murder against the disciples of the Lord, went to the high priest and asked him for letters to the synagogues at Damascus, so that if he found any who belonged to the Way, men or women, he might bring them bound to Jerusalem. Now as he was going along and approaching Damascus, suddenly a light from heaven flashed around him. He fell to the ground and heard a voice saying to him, "Saul, Saul, why do you persecute me?" He asked, "Who are you, Lord?" The reply came, "I am Jesus, whom you are persecuting. But get up and enter the city, and you will be told what you are to do." The men who were traveling with him stood speechless because they heard the voice but saw no one. Saul got up from the ground, and though his eyes were open, he could see nothing; so they led him by the hand and brought him into Damascus. For three days he was without sight, and neither ate nor drank," (Acts 9:1-9 NRSV).

Saul had glimpsed the light of truth and the shift in his understanding would change everything about him—eventually even his name.

Paul, confined to a prison cell, is singly focused and continues to do the work of Spirit as he understands that work to be. No matter his physical predicament, he is compelled to teach others to live within the borders of humility, gentleness, patience, love, peace and unity as he himself has been sequestered to a Christ directed life. Restricted by the walls of prison, his outer territory is *limited,* yet his inner terrain reaches wide and far into the realm of oneness: one with God and one with those he attempts to guide in the Christ way.

Rather than accept the ways of the world as his reality, detention in a prison cell is not his focus or his truth. He is "the prisoner in the Lord." His *cell* is an inward dwelling place that *restrains* him from wallowing in his ego and prevents him from exercising his personal will. As "prisoner in the Lord" he has surrendered his former way of being, thinking, doing and now lives as a willing detainee of Christ. A prison cell holds his body, but his true *imprisonment* is to an unwavering commitment to do the will of God as he discerns it, and to do the will of God only. But what happened to Saul that the man Paul would have such steadfast passion? He had seen the light of truth, he had heard the voice of the Lord speak to him, he was without sight for three days, and yes, he had gone without food or drink for three days as well. Surely these things would affect anyone greatly. But one more thing happened for Saul that would give rise to the relentless, unyielding passion that would come to define the man Paul.

> "While they were worshiping the Lord and fasting, the Holy Spirit said, "Set apart for me Barnabas and Saul for the work to which I have called them." Then after fasting and praying they laid their hands on them and sent them off," (Acts 13:2-3 NRSV).

A few verses after the above referenced scripture, Saul is thereafter referred to as Paul. His name change symbolizes a significant spiritual transformation. The man Paul who refers to himself as "prisoner in the Lord" is not acting on his personal ego or personal strength or will. He is living his life under a call to serve. God has given him a specific assignment. The Holy Spirit has revealed to him a purpose for being and has "set him apart" for a divine assignment. Through prayer and fasting, Paul did an inner work that allowed him to answer the call.

The call of Spirit can land in our hearts in a variety of ways and through unparalleled predicaments and circumstances. In fact each person who receives the call of Spirit will have their own unique "road to Damascus experience." The call invites us to journey through a state of conversion where we are compelled to do the work that Spirit reveals as our own. To embrace the journey before us, Spirit advocates that we submit to a new life, exercising restraint from dragging our ego mind-set through the passageway of transformation.

The call of Spirit no matter how dramatic or not, captures the personal ego in a moment of pure grace as the ego yields itself in complete surrender. From that time forward, great discipline is required to avoid the temptation of allowing the ego to reemerge and interfere with our new walk of faith. The call of Spirit "offers" entrance into a unique sanctuary where we live and receive our daily disposition "… The words that I speak to you I do not speak on My own authority; but the Father who dwells in Me does the works," (John 14:10 NKJV).

If we fully surrender to the call of Spirit, we have accepted the "offer." Then, we shall find ourselves captive to ways of being that free us from the common attitudes of ego driven behaviors. In complete submission to the call of Spirit, Paul accepts the circumstances that befall him. He does not cast blame, pass harsh judgments or complain. He is compelled to live in truth, and to embrace a life committed to "making every effort to maintain the unity of the Spirit in the bond of peace." His trust in Christ never waivers. Anchored in the call of Spirit, set apart for a unique assignment, Paul will not be moved by outer circumstances and their appearances. So, although confined to a prison cell, he possesses a freedom most people only imagine possible.

The Call to Serve on the Board of Trustees

It's relatively easy for most people to accept that a spiritual leader receives a "call" from Spirit as did those we read about in the bible. From as early as children in Sunday school, we may have heard the story of Moses who God spoke to from a burning bush, or Joshua his successor who was divinely chosen to lead the children of Israel into the promise land; and surely the New Testament presentation of Jesus' birth unveils him as one who God specifically called and selected into spiritual leadership. So it is generally expected that spiritual leaders would receive a call, a sign, a vision—something from Spirit which then becomes their purpose and passion to fulfill the assignment God has put on the leader's heart. In fact, congregants want to know, and need to believe that just like biblical characters of old, so too did their spiritual leader receive a call. The event may not have been as dramatic as standing in front of a burning bush or being temporarily blinded by a light on a road named Damascus; but congregants want to know that something happened in the life of their leader where Spirit gave them a mission, vision, purpose that involved helping and supporting others on their spiritual journey.

For the spiritual leader the call may evolve through Spirit-led ways of self-discovery, the urge to teach, the joy of living a Spirit-centered life, a desire to be of service to make a difference in the lives of others and the world. Additionally, the spiritual leader is willing to extensively train through years of seminary training strengthening the personal and professional development that positions the leader to receive credentialing by the body that has the role to ordain spiritual leaders for a particular denomination. Serving on the board for the spiritual leader is part of his or her role for the assignment as spiritual and chief organizational leader. Generally, a seat at the boardroom table for the spiritual leader comes with the position unless the bylaws dictate some other arrangement.

The call for members of the board may also evolve overtime in Spirit-led ways of self-discovery and personal growth. However, the difference is in the commitment to undertake the prescribed seminary training to receive the ordination to perform as the spiritual head of the center. Board members gain a seat at the board table usually by appointment or an election process; however, it is detailed in the organizational bylaws.

The call to serve on the board is a process, and at every point along that process attention to detail is meaningful and valuable for a board member's overall quality of engagement in serving.

So, for Paul to beg the spiritual leader to "lead a life worthy of the calling to which you have been called" would not cause us to raise an eyebrow. A certain level of integrity, character, morals and ideals are expected as an important part of spiritual leadership. In the ordination process a code of ethics or oath of conduct is taken, and we fully expect the leader to abide by that standard.

Paul's message to the Ephesian church was to all the leaders in the church. The call of Spirit is not limited to the leader but also extends to those who make the commitment to serve alongside the spiritual leader. Those others will be the members in the community who demonstrate a willingness to follow the spiritual path of living, abide by the teachings, desire to serve God with a sincere heart, love what the community stands for, and desire health, growth, and well-being for the overall ministry. But one more thing is required, one must accept Spirit's "offer" by saying YES!

Just as the spiritual leader experiences an inner divine pull, so too can we expect those who work in close proximity with them to have a call to serve. It may be an inner nudge, push, pull, jolt toward greater service, but it should be a call nevertheless. Those who serve with the spiritual leader will be those who on some level, have said, "Yes" or "Here I am." That affirmative response opens the way for acceptance of the call to serve and begins the formation of the personal contract with Spirit.

The Offer, The Invitation

When Jesus began his ministry, he called twelve to serve alongside him. They would be under his training and, because much would be expected of them Jesus framed their "call" to serve as an invitation, an offer.

> 18 As he walked by the Sea of Galilee, he saw two brothers, Simon, who is called Peter, and Andrew his brother, casting a net into the sea—for they were fishermen. [19] And he said to them, "Follow me, and I will make you fish for people." [20] Immediately they left their nets and followed him. [21] As he went from there, he saw two other brothers, James son of Zebedee and his brother John, in the boat with their father Zebedee, mending their nets, and he called them. [22] Immediately they left the boat and their father and followed him. (Matthew 4:18-22).

Surely these men had the option to stay where they were and continue in their lifestyle and occupation. In fact, careful study of the scriptures reveals that after the first "invitation" to serve, the disciples Peter, Andrew, James and John went back to being fisherman for a while. Their "Yes" to his invitation, was received as an "offer." Although they immediately left their boats, and families to follow Jesus, they had not yet made a commitment.

For a time, they watched, observed, followed from a distance with Jesus' offer in their hearts and minds. The inner movement of Spirit had not taken hold completely, so a full acceptance came over time. It was when Jesus demonstrated an amazing fishing catch in the same waters where the disciples had fished for hours catching nothing that they were ready to commit. This time, the scripture says, "they left everything and followed him," (Luke 5:11). The key here is "they left everything." They had to leave behind all they thought they knew. Teachable, willing to serve and ready to follow a new spiritual path they committed to serve by following Jesus.

Now, in Jesus' day the disciples would have been a full-service ministry team. While all were called into spiritual growth and transformation through Jesus' teachings, some were equipped and assigned to responsibilities likened to our modern-day board of trustees.

The "offer" from a spiritual community to serve on the board is most likely the part where someone is recommended to serve or shows an interest in serving. There are requirements to board service that are set out in the bylaws of the organization. There must be a time allowed where one has the option to accept or decline. Like the disciples, they wanted to follow Jesus but one of the requirements was "to leave everything," and at the first invitation they simply were not ready to commit.

So, the first order of preparation for board service is for the candidate to self-assess his or her interest, willingness to serve and the individual capability to fulfill the requirements. Board service may require long hours and many personal sacrifices. Members are asked to remain teachable in spiritual principles and business affairs. And, while a spiritual leader generally receives some compensation, the rewards for board members are primarily of an intrinsic value. In other words, board members must be willing to give of their time, talent and treasure for which no financial compensation is afforded. It is true that some nonprofit boards can receive a stipend of some kind, and there may be reimbursement for reasonable expenses incurred in board activities, but generally in a church, board service is a volunteer role.

Therefore, something deeper must be the instigator for one to say "Yes" to serve. There must be a magnifying force that pulls one into the realm of this high level of service in an organization whose purpose, mission and vision is of a spiritual basis. Board service is a calling. The agreement to serve means we've reviewed the offer and have made a conscious, thoughtful, prayerful decision to say "Yes." That willingness to leave everything behind means we will work with the other members so as to speak and act in one voice, singly focused and united in Spirit.

In whatever way the invitation of board service is received, we can honor the position by expecting candidates to activate their own inner guidance. The ministry leaders will prayerfully ask for members within the faith community to nominate someone or offer themselves to serve. In this way, we invoke Spirit to draw into leadership those who will be a blessing to the spiritual leader, fellow board members and the overall ministry.

The prayer is that it is a Spirit guided process. The one who says "Yes," is responding to the prayers that have been sent out in search for a willing vessel for Spirit to use in that particular ministry. We pray and trust that the candidate has felt the inner pull, a call from Spirit to serve and responded with "Here I am Lord, use me."

No One is "Just" a Board Member

Some years ago, in our church an incident developed between a member of the church and a member of the board. When the board member and I discussed forgiving the church member the response was "Hey, you're the minister, I'm just a board member." While over time there was reconciliation between the two, the board member's comment stayed with me.

If we want unity on the board, we want to make sure that all members understand the potential of their contribution and influence to the health, peace, growth and prosperity of the ministry. When the spiritual leader and board members approach and view their individual and combined leadership role as an opportunity to serve as a team formed from a divine calling for the glory of

God, for the common good of that spiritual community, unity has fertile ground upon which to take hold and grow. Charles Fillmore, cofounder of Unity School of Christianity says in the *Revealing Word*,

> Unity—Universal oneness of God, man, and all creation. The only real unity is in Spirit. It is found nowhere else because personality always strives for its own success and aims for the good of the personal man, instead of the good of all men.

Unity happens when we operate in and from Spirit, the ideal of universal oneness. Once members of the board along with the spiritual leader honor each other's place at the table as a "Yes" to the call of Spirit, we bind ourselves to Spirit's agenda, not our own. Charles Fillmore's definition of unity also tells us why Paul felt the need to raise the very consciousness of the entire leadership team by getting them to view their joint role as a call of Spirit. To be called by Spirit is to set aside personality as Fillmore states, "personality always strives for its own success and aims for the good of the personal man, instead of the good of all men."

Fillmore confirmed what Paul suggested in his message to the Ephesians: if we act on "personal" accord, we shall strive for ego driven success, making us ripe for the temptation to aim for individual good, rather than for the common good of the spiritual community. Paul gives specific examples as to the attitudes of mind from which board service can meet Spirit's call. The board sincerely attempting to operate from this level of harmony strives to work under the banner of one body, one Spirit, one hope, "one Lord, one faith, one baptism, one God and Father of all, who is above all and through all and in all," (Ephesians 4:5-6 NRSV).

Paul's idea is that the attitudes of those around the boardroom table be that of unity, peace and oneness demonstrated by first honoring the "spiritual credentialing" or the call of Spirit of each member. Second each person at the table, if indeed privileged to be "called" to serve, has the responsibility to be vigilant and intent on operating from Spirit rather than personal ego. In this way, humility, gentleness, patience and love become the expectation shared around the table. As Spirit has called together a team so shall there be evidence of its fruit.

> "By contrast, the fruit of the Spirit is love, joy, peace, patience, kindness, generosity, faithfulness, gentleness, and self-control. There is no law against such things," (Galatians 5:22-23 NRSV).

Humility

Humility's prime directive is to set aside our personality, personal will, controlling nature and pride of the flesh, in honor and recognition that there is a divine wisdom that transcends our own. Jesus left us with this important way to describe it, "Blessed are the meek, for they will inherit the earth," (Matthew 5:5). This is one of Jesus' teachings that is a bit unpopular. Many think it means we will leave ourselves wide open and appear weak to others who will *run all over us*. So, meekness is not a favorite word or ideal when we attempt to apply it on a human relations level.

However, if we look at this teaching as a method of approach to Spirit and spiritual matters, meekness becomes a reasonable idea. It simply stands to reason (to most of us) that we don't know everything, about everything, and certainly not all the time. We'd probably agree that Spirit does however know everything, about everything, and all the time. With this acknowledgement, we can at least grasp the idea of meekness when it comes to God, Spirit and Truth. Our meekness is to Spirit. We yield to God for guidance, direction, faith, all things, and in every circumstance. In his book, *Keep a True Lent*, Charles Fillmore states:

> "Jesus did not take the universe on His shoulders by affirming His self-sufficiency. He unloaded every burden and rested in the all-sufficiency of the Father. "I can of myself do nothing"; "the Father abiding in me doeth his works." This is the total denial of self—the giving up of all personal desires, claims and aims. Before man can do this successfully he must change his ideas—there must be a mental house cleaning."

He surrendered his personal will by his words "I can of myself do nothing, the Father abiding in me doeth his works." Humility! If Jesus didn't take the world on his shoulders why would we? Members around the boardroom table of a love centered organization must indeed consider the path of the Way-shower and his teachings as the manual of operation.

Saying "Yes" to board service is an admission that we will strive to position ourselves to do some mental house cleaning. We give up any individualized agendas for a seat at the table of harmony. The more we embrace the idea of being called by Spirit, the more we can accept that we are on the board to do the work and the will of Spirit. This is the mind-set of humility and demonstrates that we have an open mind to match our willing heart.

Gentleness

Gentleness comes a bit more easily if we sincerely desire to integrate humility into our mental attitude and seek to operate as a member of a spiritual team. "Let your gentleness be known to everyone. The Lord is near," (Philippians 4:5 NRSV).

Gentleness is a natural outgrowth of our character when we actively work to live a spiritual life and put our effort into being God centered. When we reach out to others in kindness with our words and actions, gentleness grows from within and is received by those around us. As we live a Spirit-led life, our compassion increases, and we find that we can give a lighter touch to misunderstandings with others. Gentleness that is the result of personal effort allows us to be more consistent in peaceful interactions. Gentleness can be learned says the master teacher: "Take my yoke upon you and learn from me, for I am gentle and humble in heart, and you will find rest for your souls. For my yoke is easy and my burden is light," (Matthew 11:29-30 NIV).

Patience

Restraint, tolerance, endurance are words that come to mind when we speak of patience. Patience can be challenging in spiritual leadership. We often want to get things done in our ministry and get them done quickly.

We may even be tempted to become disappointed with fellow board members, congregants or even the spiritual leader when things don't seem to be moving fast enough on what we want to achieve.

In our ministry, for five years we prayed, searched, held several prayer vigils, and viewed many properties before finding our right and perfect home. Many times, during the process the board felt the frustration and disappointment, and yes, so did I. We needed to do our searching and praying but with the faithful assurance that our right and perfect home would be made known to us in divine timing—patience.

When we surrender to the principle of divine order and divine timing we shall ease the anxiety of impatience. If indeed it is the will of Spirit, know that Spirit has a process by which it may manifest and a timing that is divinely associated with it. "I waited patiently for the Lord and he inclined unto me and heard my cry," (Psalm 40:1). Patience is a matter of trust—trust in the presence of God always operating under grace, truth and divine perfection. So, when we are feeling impatient and disturbed with all the emotions that surface when we are in the space of "I want this now," recite Psalm 40:1 and then breathe a sigh of relief.

"But about that day or hour no one knows, not even the angels in heaven, nor the Son, but only the Father. Be on guard! Be alert! You do not know when that time will come," (Mark 13:32-33 NIV).

Meditate on trusting God's timing. Accept that all things divine have an appointed time. When we feel impatient we have fallen into a mindset that believes "We," or "I" know what's best in a given situation, that's a good time to recall: "being confident of this, that he who began a good work in you will carry it on to completion until the day of Christ Jesus," (Phil. 1:6 NIV)

Bearing With One Another in Love
To "bear with one another in love" speaks to how we relate, interact and communicate with others. If our hearts are already set toward humility, gentleness and patience we have the makings for bearing with others in love.

To bear with each other in love does not mean we will "like" every idea or agree with every opinion. It does mean that we are willing to listen and remain open while we are hearing one another. If after listening and hearing another, we disagree or simply do not have a liking for an idea, position or plan of action, our response can still be made from a place of kindness and void of personal attacks.

To bear with one another in love recognizes that we are all children of God and have our own individual ways of expressing our unique self. Acceptance of others just the way they are, with the expectation that we too will be accepted just as we are, is a strong support for the harmony we seek.

While we accept each other as is, we have come together at the boardroom table to grow personally and as a spiritual team serving to the glory of God in a ministry we all love. Ironically this means if we are effective at the boardroom table, in some way, and over time, we shall all be changed.

To bear with one another in love, we shall support the changes in each person at the table as part of a process of growth that we all have been called to participate in. After all, we were created to grow and therefore change must happen. To bear with one another in love is to support and encourage Spirit changing all at the table from within to the outer.

Make Every Effort to Maintain the Unity of the Spirit in the Bond of Peace
On the individual level peace is a choice. If peace is a bond by which we choose to function at the boardroom table, we will need to practice peace in our individual lives. As the person we plan to be at the boardroom table will be an extension from how we are in our daily lives. To think we can pull off a "bond of peace" attitude at the boardroom table and function as "trouble maker" the rest of the month simply will not fly—and divine law will not permit it.

We *practice* peace to anchor it into our consciousness and allow it to become a habit, our action and reaction to life's circumstances. To have the intention of "making every effort" to maintain unity of the Spirit says we are conscious that we are spirit. Fillmore's words apply: "The only real unity is in Spirit." In this way our work is to exhaust every possibility in our mental and spiritual tool box rather than break the bond of peace we have with Spirit. Yes, our bond is with Spirit, so we practice and express that bond with those with whom we interact—around and beyond the boardroom table.

To make a full effort at something says if we use our options and choices with all sincerity we can affect the outcome. We have no one else to blame if we fail to reach for a word of punishment over a word of peace. At the boardroom table we all have a part in shaping the direction of the ministry. For this reason, our input into the outcomes, decisions, actions and solutions that come before the board are valuable. As partners at the boardroom table we have the power to make a difference and to do so from a consciousness of peace. "Great peace have they which love thy law: and nothing shall offend them," (Psalm 119:165).

Our outcomes do indeed depend on our thoughts, our attitude, our beliefs, words and actions. If we make *every effort* we will pray every applicable prayer, say every relevant affirmation, use every fitting scripture and put into practice every right action we know to uphold the bond of peace. To make every effort says we are willing to do whatever it takes to live in unity. "If it is possible, as far as it depends on you, live at peace with everyone," (Romans 12:18 NIV).

A Spiritual Approach to Board Service

Jesus was very meticulous in calling together his team of twelve. He was persistent, patient and prayerful in bringing the disciples together. No spiritual leader can fulfill God's mission or the work he or she is called to do alone. So, others who will offer their hearts and hands to facilitate the work, the mission, the vision would do well to acknowledge their service as a divine invitation and subsequent divine appointment. Board service can work well when we are intentional and thorough in selecting members to the board. Prayer infused in every stage of board selection from receiving nominations, applications, interviews of candidates and the vote of the congregation shall be Spirit guided.

The detail we pay to the process is not to keep anyone out, but to pave the way for the one that genuinely accepts the call of Spirit to give of their time, talent and treasure. The member who humbly receives and accepts an inner invitation of Spirit to join the leadership team will be a great blessing to the overall ministry. A spiritual approach to board service rather than coercion will provide the best opportunity for those seated at the boardroom table to make a commitment to serve in harmony and from a bond of peace.

Board service as a calling is best supported by the spiritual leader who models spiritual leadership, teaches truth, and supports the growth of each member on the board. When we read of how Paul coached the leadership team of the early church we see that he infused a standard for their actions, and the expectation that they could deliver their best to their role in the church. Paul also modeled his commitment, even from a prison cell, holding his faith and passion intact while continuing to fulfill what he discerned as his mission and purpose.

Jesus took a group of men who were already fishing and showed them how to fish for men. "And he saith unto them, Follow me, and I will make you fishers of men," (Matthew 4:19). In other words, Jesus invited a group of people who were already seeking (symbolized by their act of fishing) and through his example, teaching and direct companionship gave them the tools that would allow them to eventually go out to become teachers themselves. The spiritual leader is foremost a teacher of the truth principles, spiritual laws, teachings of Jesus Christ and other teachers of truth. The spiritual leader's position on the board is to be a Christ guided example for those who sit with him or her around the boardroom table and maintain the belief and expectation that they have been drawn together to share in a unified divine assignment.

Affirmation for Spiritual Key #1:
Our unity of purpose activates the power of Spirit to use us as a united team, a ready and willing vessel for expected and unexpected blessings.

1st Spiritual Key: PURPOSE

1. Board service is a "calling."

2. An invitation to serve is an opportunity to participate in the great assignment Spirit has for your ministry.

3. To fulfill the mission and vision of your ministry there must be unity of purpose.

- Establish and strive to function by a scripturally based Code of Conduct that is instructional as is Ephesians 4:1-6. (Reprinted in the Appendix I). It gives a clearly defined purpose and specific instructions on how to meet the purpose described. The board of trustees Code of Conduct is different from the board of trustees Code of Ethics. While the Code of Ethics is valuable and important it is different from spiritual instructions and comes later in the process of accepting board service.
- Seek out candidates for board service who are well versed in the core values, beliefs and principles upon which the ministry is founded—this will support their willingness to accept Spirit's call to serve.
- Put in extra work in preparing board candidates for what they may expect at every step in the process of selection, interview, installation, orientation and the seating at the boardroom table.

- Present board service to prospective candidates as an opportunity for greater spiritual growth through high level service in the ministry; introduce them to the Code of Conduct for your board of trustees early in the selection process.

- In every stage of board service encourage candidates and board members alike to explore their personal inspiration and motivation for board service. Following the "call of Spirit" or viewing board service as a "divine appointment" instills a sense of purpose. Purpose opens the way for acceptance of greater responsibility, and willingness toward greater accountability.

Discussion Starters for Board Bonding - Purpose

1. Describe a key experience, event, or moment in time that led you to say yes to serve on the board.

2. Describe your understanding of the spiritual purpose of the board.

3. In Ephesians 4, it says "be worthy of the calling to which you have been called," give your thoughts about this statement and how it relates to your service on the board.

4. In Ephesians 4:1-3 we read qualities of character for serving, as "humility, gentleness, patience, bearing with one another in love, making every effort to maintain the unity of the Spirit in the bond of peace." Discuss these individually and add any other personal qualities that could lead to a highly functioning board.

5. Having read in Chapter One that everyone serving on the board has answered a divine call, what can the board do more of to honor, appreciate and respect each board member's divine appointment to give of their time, talent and treasure.

The additional time we put into the assurance that every person at the table understands their roles and responsibilities at the beginning of a new board cycle, will pay off in great measure toward the overall effectiveness of the board.

Chapter Two

Spiritual Compatibility

COMMONALITY

"Therefore if *there is* any consolation in Christ, if any comfort of love, if any fellowship of the Spirit, if any affection and mercy, fulfill my joy by being like-minded, having the same love, *being* of one accord, of one mind."

--Philippians 2:1-2 (NKJV)

Like-mindedness in spiritual leadership is not thinking the same in our ideas and opinions. We each bring to the table different types of education, experience, skills, talents and abilities. In fact, we should strive for diversity of thought, perspective and different points of view. A variety of gifts, skills, experiences and talents are important to be a clear vessel that Spirit may fulfill the great assignment of your ministry. Here we must realize the value of diversity at the table. Each member around the table brings their own uniqueness, a valued perspective. It will be our differences that will provide Spirit with a full assortment of ordinary people divinely drawn together as an extraordinary team through which to work.

The like-mindedness around the table is in the heart and spirit
of love we have for truth, the teachings of Jesus Christ as we
understand and interpret them, and the spiritual laws and principles
that are the foundation of the ministry we all love. When we
embrace the Christ presence as our commonality, we set the table
of leadership with a powerful utensil—harmony. All who are called
and guided to sit at the table can then receive into their heart the
great emotion of human connectedness—the feeling of oneness with
each other, and a oneness with Spirit. In his book *Jesus Christ Heals*,
Charles Fillmore states,

> Jesus had a grasp of divine ideas, and if we believe in and follow
> Him we shall come into the Christ state of mind. We become
> like-minded by entering into the absolute Mind. In the absolute
> Mind there is only harmony.

Like-mindedness has its makings from the kinship we share as children
of God, joint heirs as brothers and sisters to Jesus Christ. Our meeting
place with Spirit is Mind; our meeting place with each other is also Mind.
Our natural kinship connects us one to another. Our like-mindedness is
our "divine" commonality. Paul suggests those who are striving to walk
the spiritual path, have a divine kinship that unites one to another as
"brothers and sisters in Christ."

> "Now I appeal to you, brothers and sisters, by the name of
> our Lord Jesus Christ, that all of you be in agreement and that
> there are no divisions among you, but that you be united in the
> same mind and the same purpose," (1 Corinthians 1:10 NRSV).

Now growing up as a young girl in a family of eight children—four
boys and four girls, there were always disagreements and much division
among us. I can see why Paul says, "brothers and sisters, by the name
of our Lord Jesus Christ." For left to our experience of how brothers
and sisters behave from a purely human perspective, we may find
ourselves reflecting on the kind of division that comes with fights,
arguments, retaliation and in our family, all followed by the punishment
of a strict parent.

Most of us had our first experiences with division in relationships from early childhood family dynamics. The sibling relationship is often where we had our first exposure to what happens when we disagree with others. For those who did not have brothers and sisters, our early relationship lessons may have come from friends or, simply from taking notes from mom and dad. Our mental references may include how to fight, argue, defend and protect ourselves but may not have provided the tools of forgiveness, reconciliation and the humility to be the first to apologize. The playbook we use as adults, when we disagree with others or when others disagree with us, may bring flashbacks of unpleasant confrontations we had or witnessed as children. If we did indeed come from a family where there was lots of love, peace and harmony going on all the time, our experience in the world of work may have been our introduction to the "every man for himself" mentality that is present in many work environments.

No matter how we arrived at our skills and abilities for facing disagreements with others, if our foundation is not of a spiritual approach, an awareness of divine love, an inner recognition of a divine kinship, or as Paul frames it, "by the name of our Lord Jesus Christ," then disagreements will be solved by attempting to apply purely human methods, and that approach will give rise to the very division Paul warns us against.

So, when Paul addresses "brothers and sisters," he is speaking of the divine family that we are to one another. He is addressing the ultimate love that we share as children of God, brothers and sisters in Christ. He speaks to our natural highest nature of love which links us in the same mind and purpose. He addresses the Corinthians in a way that reminds them of who they really are, brothers and sisters, the offspring and expression of God. And as we seek harmony at the boardroom table, we will do well to remember that we are the offspring of the one presence and power we call God, Spirit, Divine Love, Mind. In the divine family there is room for a variety of methods and opinions by which we may grasp the ideals that steer us clear of division. Our spiritual compatibility rests in the ideal that although of many differences, we are "brothers and sisters by the name of our Lord Jesus Christ."

It is likely that whatever process we learned growing up, as a means of achieving common ground in relationships may not have reached Jesus's approach: "agree with thy adversary quickly" or "pray for those who persecute you" or "forgive seventy times seven." This quality of relationship compatibility takes work and lots of on-going practice. A seat at the boardroom table is a great place to practice Jesus's teachings on relationship building and thereby discover that we are alike in more ways than we have known.

When we honor that we are all legitimate members of the divine family we are positioned to acknowledge and remember our heritage: goodness. God has no illegitimate children. We are all created in the image and likeness of God. We are told in the first book of the bible "And God saw everything that he had made, and, behold, it was very good," (Genesis 1:31). This declaration is made early in the scriptures because it is a foundational core to all harmonious relationships. This is the like-mindedness from which we must live, grow and evolve, personally and professionally. If we find ourselves at the table of leadership for an organization whose mission is to draw forth the goodness in others, our work must start from our connectedness, our commonality—our practice of goodness. "Surely goodness and mercy shall follow me all the days of my life…" (Psalm 23:6 NRSV). As a board anchored in this spiritual compatibility, we build goodness into the fabric of our board culture and goodness will be embedded in our interactions with each other and all we do together.

Installation—Public Acceptance of the Call to Serve

The installation ritual is an opportunity to highlight the existence and value of spiritual compatibility on the board. This can be done as a celebration of an important and sacred event. For some who join the board it is their first real commitment to serving in a leadership capacity where the mission, vision and methods of operation are spiritual. They may have served on their homeowners association board or a board of a corporation or community board but never with a spiritually-guided team of people committed to tithe of their time, talent and treasure as part of that commitment.

An installation ceremony of the members of the board before the congregation has several purposes and benefits. It binds the members of the board and the spiritual leader together in a goal of unification—one mind, one purpose. To be single-minded in purpose gives the board its first assignment. This oneness re-affirms the consciousness by which the entire board is expected to function. To stand together, of one mind and of the same purpose emits a powerful vibrational energy of kinship, brothers and sisters of the highest ideal—with each other, one in Christ.

The installation process bestows a blessing on the board and spiritual leader as a God inspired, carefully crafted leadership team for the overall good, health, growth and prosperity of the spiritual community.

I use the idea of *ceremony* as it marks the launch of a major event. From days of old, festivals and celebrations, large and small, mark an important date to highlight some great thing God had done. Celebration allows for a moment of gratitude while stirring hope for what God is expected to unveil in the future. In modern times our own inauguration ceremonies for leaders are well planned and elegantly done. Again, it marks a time of celebration of what God has unveiled through our consciousness in the present and for future expectation of success, health, growth and abundant good.

Most spiritual communities celebrate the installation of a new spiritual leader. And many faith communities mark that installation time for future anniversary celebrations for the spiritual leader. I am a believer that the anniversary of the spiritual leader should be acknowledged, in some way, each year and in a larger way at five, ten, fifteen, twenty, etc. years. It is important to provide the community with an opportunity to show its appreciation for the spiritual leader and it is important for the spiritual leader to receive recognition for their leadership. This simple process of appreciation and recognition can be instrumental in demonstrating the congregation's value of its spiritual leadership and provide an opportunity for the expression of gratitude. The congregation that expresses sincere gratitude improves and widens the path for blessings to manifest.

Just as we celebrate the installation of a new spiritual leader so too will we benefit when we celebrate each new board. We acknowledge board service separate and apart from the spiritual leader's installation or annual anniversary celebrations. Although the annual installation of the entire board includes the spiritual leader as a member of the board, these are two different celebrations. The annual board installation has several important valuations:

- It introduces to the congregation a unified team of leaders in whom they have entrusted the overall administration and well-being of the community as a whole. The visual of the team standing together should refresh their hope, faith and trust that Spirit is at work in the ministry.

- It gives the board and minister the opportunity to experience what it feels like to be recognized as a unified team. That feeling can establish a deeper desire to maintain that feeling of unity.

- It allows for the board and spiritual leader to receive the blessing of the congregation in the matters and affairs of the ministry.

- It gives the community an opportunity to express their appreciation for this committed group of volunteers.

- It provides the opportunity for existing board members to renew their commitment, while allowing new board members to receive a blessing for their new commitment to serve.

- It is a teachable moment for the congregation to learn more about what the board does and their role.

Consider the installation an investment in the intention of a fresh start for the leadership. Each beginning can set in motion great things to come for the individuals who give of their time, talent and treasure and for the overall ministry. The Board installation is an opportunity to make all things new and fresh. Let it mark a time of celebration for a great new beginning for the entire spiritual community. Let there be joyful recognition of the team Spirit has assembled for a mighty purpose. "Therefore what God has joined together, let no one separate," (Mark 10:9 NIV).

Orientation to Serving from the Call of Spirit

The orientation is an opportunity to emphasize the value, importance and responsibilities of the board to the ongoing health, growth and prosperity of the ministry. When there is a clear understanding of the roles and responsibilities of every person at the boardroom table, harmony has a chance. New board members will have a good overall experience when they understand what is expected of them as well as what is expected of the spiritual leader. Anything less than clear, definable instruction and discussion of what is expected, of all members of the board including the spiritual leader, is a set up for misunderstanding in the future.

As I look back at my experience with our boards over many years, the members who did not either perform their best or embrace the board experience as a great one, were those who were not clear on the role and responsibilities of the board of a spiritual community. I noticed too that without clear instruction on fulfilling their role they wandered into areas that were outside the scope of board responsibility. So, for me, orientation is important for the entire board to go through together every year.

While the orientation is traditionally the time to cover the governance aspects of board service, we can infuse the development of our like-mindedness into the process. For example, one the board's foundational roles is to be champions, protectors and caretakers of the mission, vision and values. For, this reason the mission deserves more than a mere mention as is so often the case. Here is an opportunity for sharing and discussion for the potential of bonding board members to each other, the mission, vision and values and the community it has committed to serve. When board members have an opportunity to share their personal story regarding the meaning of mission, vision and values, they voice how they came to have a seat at the boardroom table. This is an important point. The board member who moves beyond the thinking I've heard so many times which says "Oh, I'm only on the board because no one else would run," or "I just want to know what goes on behind closed doors in the church," or "I need to help get things straightened out, they don't know what they're doing." All of which may be true on the surface, but until we go deeper into why and how we are seated at the table of this high-level form of ministry leadership, we have not discovered our true spiritual purpose for being there and established the strongest motivator to give their best in the process. By sharing a portion of our spiritual journey, we claim out seat at the table. We own the consciousness to sit in oneness with others whose lives have been impacted by a cause and mission that binds those who have been called to serve. Commonality.

Commonality lowers the invisible barriers that can block the development of a culture that invites listening to one another, willingness to share from the heart and the joy we can glean from having open, sincere discussions. Orientation gives us the opportunity and privilege to establish honest communication that will subsequently allow for a willingness to engage in harmonious discussions on all topics related to the ministry.

In the ministry, we used the board orientation session to review the roles and responsibilities of board service together as a full board. We discussed, asked questions, regarding any concerns, etc. The entire board participates as one unit in a "self-training" experience where we prepare to work together in harmony. This does not mean we didn't from time to time have outside training or board enrichment. However, orientation is our time to build rapport, establish a connection and discover and anchor our spiritual compatibility. We practice working together around roles and responsibilities and it sets a tone for how we will function for the year ahead—discussing, sharing, questioning and working through concerns and solutions. On many occasions (not all) asked exiting board members to sit in on the orientation of new board members to offer their insights, wisdom, prayers and support. There have been times when this has been appropriate and effective.

I am not attempting to downplay the importance of covering the governance material traditionally covered during the orientation. I am suggesting here that we cover all of what can help build a strong board. I think of this approach as setting the tone for governance and member commonality to be the drivers behind an effective board. Orientation can be an opportunity for board members to admit their spiritual journey into their board service and acknowledge the personal and professional rewards thereof.

Having set the tone of commonality, and connectedness, we can have a more open, honest, broad minded discussion on the important topics under the heading of governance. We stated above the board's responsibility regarding the mission, vision and values. Yes, this is a grand place to start, then we move to the mindset of the fiduciary responsibility. In other words, the board members must approach all that is to be done as the responsible and accountable body for the ministry with the kind of care that is said to be reasonable and prudent. This means they give the kind of care, attention, focus as one would give their own life and affairs. All this plus a willingness to abide by the all laws and rules applicable to nonprofit organizations and any specific compliances for religious and 501 (c) (3) legal structures. The board then, must delve into and have a good understanding of the legal, financial and corporate responsibilities.

There should be a specific study on each of the roles and responsibilities beyond what is mentioned in this book. I give here ten key accountabilities to remember in service on the board:

I.   Board members should be champions for the mission, vision and values. Regularly use these as the standard of motivation behind decisions and plans. Place them where they can be seen at every board meeting,

II.   Read the bylaws as a group once a year - during the orientation is ideal. This is the board's guidebook, so it helps for the board to know what it says. Review them periodically to determine if amendments and revisions are needed. Doing this annually can be an important part of the board's self-evaluation, asking for example "how well did we follow our bylaws this past year?"

III.   Structure Board meeting time to be effective in covering all necessary business affairs, but also infuse opportunities for the meeting to be uplifting and inspiring. Perhaps there could be a bit of fun infused. Who says board service has to be lacking in laughter and joy?

IV.   Use the gifts afforded religious and spiritual organizations-collective prayer, spiritual practices and sacred ceremony. Use these gifts often and lavishly.

V.   Provide regular training, development and enrichment for the ongoing education and growth for board members and the board as a whole. An annual retreat can be a great way to do this kind of work.

VI.   Share commitments through established and signed Codes of Conduct, Statements addressing Ethics, Confidentiality, Conflicts of Interest.

VII.   Develop well thought-out requirements for board service. Introduce candidates to the requirements early in the nomination process. Factor in board composition into the recruitment process: think diversity of skills, talents, experience as well as age, gender, race, sexual orientation, differently-abled, etc.

VIII.   Take financial oversight seriously. Regularly improve the board's knowledge on financial matters.

IX.   Annually review the board's roles and responsibilities. Work together to support each other in practicing and fulfilling them.

X.   Develop a strategic plan with annual goals for the board to work toward. Remember, change is a constant, but you'll still need a plan.

This is not meant to be an exhaustive list or in-depth explanation of the board's full roles and responsibilities. But it will set the board on a sound foundation of the duties of service.

The orientation can give the board an opportunity to establish methods of discussion and operation that lend themselves to build, develop and operate as a highly effective board. Orientation is the first board convening, so use it to establish a positive impression on new board members. It is a good time to establish assurances that spiritual principles can and will be active in the boardroom along with fulfilling the governance issues required by the board.

Election of Officers

The ministry will be bound by its own set of policies, procedures and by-laws, so I am speaking to "attitude" and "generalities" regarding overall board service and officer roles. The organization's bylaws should give greater detail into these roles.

The board of trustees of a ministry has the challenge of making two hats, serve one purpose. As trustees we are responsible to oversee the funds and assets of the ministry and to assure that the ministry operates under good stewardship. Additionally, the board must adhere to certain legal, accounting and ethical guidelines as established by governmental authority. However, at the same time trustees make the commitment to follow the spiritual path of discernment, decision making and divine right implementation. All board members need a full understanding of the governmental responsibilities of the board as well as practical knowledge of spiritual principles taught in the ministry they serve.

Officers have the added responsibility of being the ones who will "sign on the dotted line" for whatever legal documents the ministry has need to confirm through signature. Officers are generally signatories on bank and financial accounts. While they sign their own name, they sign on behalf of the entire board for the benefit of the ministry.

When we select officers for the positions on the board we want to do three very important things.

One, make the selection a prayerful choice. Before elections, pray about the decision individually and as a board. A prayerful decision will help avoid a popularity contest for the officer positions. As bonded as we may be in peace, and as committed as we may be to harmony at the table, officers who do not meet the responsibilities of their role can be a great disruption to the process of getting things done that need to be done.

Two, assure that the member understands the added role and increased responsibility of the office before they accept it. Assure there is an understanding that increased responsibility may require an officer to act individually on a matter, but the action should be one decided upon as part of a board decision.

Three, officers should bring to the role some qualification for the office to which they are elected. Here again, we may be creating more work and weight on the other members who may need to jump in and "take up the slack" when an officer does not meet the responsibilities.

Treasurer

The role of treasurer requires attention to detail. No matter the level of involvement in preparing financial statements or not, the treasurer who has an eye for detail will be a great asset to assuring the financial policies and management operations are handled in an ethical, legal, orderly and efficient way. All trustees are responsible for financial oversight however the treasurer is the point person. A treasurer may not have all the answers but knows enough to ask questions of whoever can provide the best and most adequate picture of the finances.

Secretary

The role of secretary has the great responsibility of assuring that the Minutes are prepared with as much accuracy as possible. Sometimes there is a tendency to view the secretary as a note taker. However, the minutes of a corporation – profit and non-profit constitute a legal document and should be prepared with great accuracy. Should there ever be legal issues, the Minute Book may become the board's most important official record and history of details and facts. Also in an audit the Certified Public Accountant (CPA) who performs the audit will rely on the ministry for accurate information in the Minutes.

Vice-president

The vice-president or vice chair is like the understudy in a great play. They must always be ready to jump in where the president has a need for support. The communication between president and vice is important if board operations are to flow smoothly.

President or Chairperson

I saved the president or chairperson (hereafter referred to as board chair), of the board for last as this role requires great responsibility for overall board effectiveness and includes an active healthy working relationship with the spiritual leader. This officer holds the specific role of encouraging members of the board, to work as a team, to honor the commitment of giving of time, talent and treasure, and to accept accountability to the members of the ministry.

Spiritual leader as a Member of the Board

The spiritual leader as a member of the board, of course, is to be the spiritual head of the board just as he or she is for the overall ministry. In all that is done at the boardroom table the spiritual leader inspires and promotes the guidance of Spirit as the method of operation, along with the secular legal, accounting and ethical functions required by nonprofit boards. The spiritual leader has a seat at the table to uphold, represent and encourage the use and implementation of the teachings, principles and truths upon which the ministry is founded. If the spiritual leader is also the Chief Executive Officer (CEO) with responsibility for the oversight of the day-to-day administrative operations his or her purpose at the table, serves to report to the board relevant updates on issues and affairs facing the ministry.

Spiritual Leader and Board Chair

The board chair and spiritual leader are in two positions that are linked in such close connection to the success of the ministry this discussion deserves its own section.

The board chair and the spiritual leader have a great opportunity to set the tone of unity for the entire board, if they are both willing to act with "one accord." Time spent building a professional working relationship through communication, integrity, mutual respect and kindness will go a long way toward creating a bond of peace that will show up at the boardroom table as harmony and the possibility for synergy to happen.

One of the challenges that can present itself in this relationship is that both have positions of "power" in the ministry. Power not balanced with humility, compassion, wisdom and a willingness to listen and hear others is a disaster in and of itself. So, when there are two personalities with "power" over the same cause, each with a turf to protect, a struggle can easily emerge. I am reminded of a quote by Abraham Lincoln: "Nearly all men can stand adversity, but if you want to test a man's character, give him power." Even if both parties have a great sense of self-knowledge, other leadership qualities and a sincere desire to benefit the cause, there is something about "power" that can tempt either or both toward some form of abuse.

Here are a few ideas to help foster and promote good communication while nurturing harmony and peace in this all-important relationship:

- Spiritual leader and board chair prepare the agenda for the board meeting together. This helps to assure that all issues are addressed and included for information and attention. Agenda items can then be discussed between the two in advance—not to force agreement on issues, but rather to provide an approach to items on the agenda that will focus on what is in the best interest of the overall ministry. By discussing issues in advance, many times differences can be worked out in an agreeable manner. It can also be an opportunity to clarify where disagreement exists before presenting it to the full board. What we want to avoid is dragging raw differences of opinion to the table in ways that stir contention or compel board members to take sides.

- A weekly update call between the two serves to fulfill a commitment to ongoing communication. Many times, misunderstandings arise simply out of not being informed, not being kept in the loop or not being updated as circumstances evolve and change. Communication can diffuse an issue before it gathers any traction or help avoid a challenge altogether.

- Collaboration on ideas to be brought before the board or exchanging opinions on matters affecting the ministry will help to elevate ideas toward success as well as serve the development of respect between the two. This requires both to be willing to set aside pride, egoism and perceived power in exchange for humility and a willingness to maintain peace and harmony. Respect between the spiritual leader and chair is a two-way street—an important path to effectiveness.

Our board functioned at its best when this interconnected relationship was carefully, lovingly, intentionally attended to, and nourished. A good authentic rapport between these two positions can be the board's greatest strength and its strongest asset to getting the intended things done harmoniously on behalf of the ministry.

Affirmation for Spiritual Key #2:

We celebrate our commonality by honoring the individual and unique perspectives Spirit has gathered together at our leadership table to fulfill a shared mission, vision and set of core values.

2ⁿᵈ Spiritual Key: COMMONALITY

1. Craft the installation, orientation and board trainings as opportunities to bind the board together in commonality, like-mindedness and unity of purpose.

2. Uniqueness and diversity have a powerful place in magnifying the energy of a Spirit-guided team.

3. Discovering the similarities of what appears as difference helps to set the stage of common ground—a harmonious place from which to grow and govern together.

- At the installation ceremony, before the congregation, have someone who has a strong prayer consciousness (a chaplain, a member of your prayer ministry, or a long time elder who is greatly respected within the community) to "speak words of love, peace, harmony, divine guidance and wisdom" over the entire board.

- Devise ways, rituals and strategies to support every board member in practicing and modeling their like-mindedness while sharing in the common bond of board service. I have used many rituals in the past including these two:

   #1 I used this long before the rose ceremony of a popular television show. Start with an equal number of roses to the number of members on the board. An appointed person from the congregation will come and offer a rose to each member asking something like: "_____ (name) will you accept this rose as a symbol of your love for God, truth, this ministry and the members of this spiritual community?" The board member then agrees and accepts the rose. When we use different colors of roses, or different types of flowers, we display the beauty of diversity. The visual of the board presented before the congregation as a beautiful bouquet of diverse flowers is a positive affirmation in and of itself. A congregational blessing may be done to close the installation allowing everyone to participate.

 # 2:   As part of our board installation each member including the minister selects from a basket of prayerfully selected scriptures, inspirational words or one of the twelve powers, as ascribed to Jesus' twelve disciples (faith, love, strength, etc.). We call these our "spiritual attributes" for the year. Each board member then commits to hold the intention and spiritual space for whatever they have selected from the basket on behalf of the entire board and for the ministry. Thereafter the scripture, inspirational word or faculty of mind is read by the board member at each board meeting as an intention and assurance that the consciousness represented by their statement has a place, presence and seat at the boardroom table.

• Post the scripture Ephesians 4:1-6 or your board's Code of Conduct where it shall not be forgotten. Recite it together at board meetings—consider putting it at the top of the Board Agenda, on place cards in front of each member or on a poster in the boardroom. The idea is to keep the idea in mind that each member has answered the call of Spirit, and that there is an expectation associated with it—a commonality in our willingness to serve.

• Use board activities as teachable moments for the congregation to have a better understanding of the board's role. This may be helpful in the next search for new board members.

Discussion Starters for Board Bonding – Commonality

1. Discuss a personal experience where you felt the value and importance of the mission, vision and specific values in your own life.

2. Name three things that all board members have in common. (Be willing to go beyond the obvious, dig deeper in your communication with each other).

3. Name some of the differences on the board that contribute to and expand the board's perspectives and views (example: age, gender, race, etc.).

4. Discuss ideas that could build greater connections among and between members of the board.

5. Just for fun, use your collective imaginations for the following exercise: Your board is to create an "imaginary" delicious salad. Pretend each board member represents a different ingredient, what ingredient would you be? Why? After making your imaginary salad discuss the diversity of the ingredients and the commonality of all ingredients as they work together to add to the goal of making a delicious tasting salad. What lessons were revealed from this exercise?

Genuine harmony reveals itself in greater measure, around the boardroom table, when trust is present—trust in Spirit first, then trust in each other.

Chapter Three

Building Trust,
Inviting Harmony

TRUST

"One day Jesus was praying in a certain place. When he finished, one of his disciples said to him, 'Lord, teach us to pray, just as John taught his disciples.'"
--Luke 11:1 (NIV)

Behind every question there is a statement. When the disciples asked Jesus to teach them to pray they were saying something like, *We want to see and witness grand results from our prayers*, or perhaps something like, *We want to feel the joy of God using us to bring forth good in the lives of those for whom we pray.*

On another occasion, the disciples went to Jesus disappointed that they could not heal a boy who was possessed by an impure spirit. "And when he was come into the house, his disciples asked him privately, 'Why could not we cast him out?' And he said unto them, 'This kind can come forth by nothing, but by prayer and fasting,'" (Mark 9:28-29).

Herein is a major difference between serving on the board of the homeowner's association, local school board or the board of a for-profit company. Credit for any success in the secular community goes to the board members themselves, the CEO, or perhaps a consultant hired to "make things happen." After many strategy meetings, brainstorming sessions and political maneuvers the board and CEO get all the praise for their expertise in business, finance and great organizational strategies.

Boards that serve from a spiritual mission may also have strategy meetings, brainstorming sessions and yes, even some political maneuvering: however, because we have been prayerful during the processes, claimed the guidance of Spirit and used our faith as our driving force, the praise for the success goes to Spirit. The board members and the spiritual leader pray together regarding the affairs of the ministry and when the guidance, answers and direction is revealed, of our human selves we take credit only for following Spirit.

Board members of a spiritual community need to see and witness results from prayer, want to support the ministry in prayer, and desire to feel the joy of God using them to bring forth good to the community they so lovingly serve. If board members are not actively experiencing answered prayer at work in the ministry, they can easily fall into performing as a secular board.

So, while the board members may not say with their words, "teach us to pray," serving on the board will lend itself to lessons in the practice of prayer and other spiritual principles. The major role of the spiritual leader serving on the board is to lead in spiritual matters and thereby open the way to connect spiritual practices with conventional business methods. The spiritual leader has a prime opportunity and responsibility to model, promote, encourage and teach how a spiritual approach to material systems can be utilized in executing the affairs of the ministry. The reliance on prayer at the board level will have dual benefits. As the consciousness of prayer is expanded on the personal level so will it bring good results for the ministry as well.

Praying together as a board, positions the members for agreement, and collaboration. We harness a great strength when we collectively center ourselves on God, Christ, Spirit, Truth. The process itself binds us together in unity.

Board Consciousness Matters

When a board operates with "one accord," Spirit has a willing and powerful vessel to use to fulfill the mission of the ministry. "Again, I say unto you, that if two of you shall agree on earth as touching anything that they shall ask, it shall be done for them of my Father which is in heaven. For where two or three are gathered together in my name, there am I in the midst of them," (Matthew 18:19-20).

The idea that the consciousness of those seated at the table of spiritual leadership matters is often an under-utilized gift. I believe this scripture reveals what is sometimes a missed opportunity available to the board of trustees: "For where two or
three are gathered together in my name, there am I in the midst of them." The scripture reminds the board of a spiritual teaching that allows for high quality decision making.

When the board is gathered together, they have the choice to be a receptive vehicle for divine guidance to energize their deliberations. This teaching becomes magnified for our spiritual community when the leadership team functions as one in mind, one in spirit, one in truth, and one with the divine ideals within the mission, vision and values of the church. To utilize this gift is to become one with the divine where all problems are solvable, every question has a divine answer, and every difficulty can be overcome harmoniously. When we are centered in harmony, focused on bringing forth Spirit's plan of good, we claim access to the highest wisdom available and poised for divine guidance in the process.

Once we come to admit that there is a tremendous gift in the pooling of our highest mind power, we harness a great resource granted in spiritual leadership. While for-profit boards may not have specific spiritual teachings and tools to use in their deliberations, a faith-based board does. So, the charge is this: use your faith. Use the teachings of your faith in this high-level form of service. To not use our spiritual teachings puts us out-of-sync with the purpose for which our organization exists. Boards get to bring the ideal that *God is mightier than circumstance* to the boardroom. We get to bring our prayerful hearts to every decision, choice, discussion and policy we set. Together, we can take an extra moment to come into alignment with Spirit, truth, our teachings and allow that level of collective collaboration to drive us toward the power harnessed by agreement, harmony and operating with one accord. Yes, good governance must be adhered to and attended to from a consciousness of harmony.

This harmony does not come overnight. It does not come with one board retreat. It does not come with one good training session. The work of the board is to build, grow and expand the consciousness of the board as an ongoing effort. Expanding consciousness is a steady effort, year after year, board cycle after board cycle. The board will need to be in constant recruitment and cultivation mode. As board members complete their terms and new members step onto the board, a culture of harmony, working with one accord and exercising spiritual principles as the method for *getting things done* must carry forward. In the board's list of requirements, this type of statement is beneficial: *a willingness to work in harmony as a spiritual team with the spiritual leader and fellow members of the board.* Anything less, will open the door for distractions away from the mission, vision and values that are the driving purpose behind all that the board stands for.

Ongoing education, training, and retreats is essential. As the world is in such a state of change, boards must work to stay abreast of issues that affect their organization. We want to strive to be proactive rather than spend the bulk of our time and energy reacting to circumstances or putting out fires started in personality wars and power struggles.

Just as we get our annual check-up with our primary care professional, the board needs to submit to check-ups as well. Your doctor will ask lots of questions about how you're doing, follow up with a few tests and make recommendations for going forward in good health. The board should do the same thing with periodic self-assessments, evaluations, check-ups and check-in's. These can be administered as part of annual trainings and retreats and are valuable for ongoing health, growth, strength of the board experience.

One of the reasons I decided to write this book is because I believe, those of us who are called and guided to serve on the board our spiritual community, want to make a meaningful difference in the place where we pray, meditate, grow, celebrate and connect with like-minded friends and family. And, while board service is a great commitment requiring lots of time and effort, it can be one of the ways we serve that can bring us joy, and a deep sense of personal value and fulfillment. In the boardroom, we have a real chance to put our unique skills, talents, experience and expertise to use where the reward of helping others is its own reward, and so worth whatever sacrifices we choose to make.

My prayer for every board is that you enjoy the journey. It is always a blessing when I meet with boards who recognize the value of acknowledging and celebrating their successes and the achievement made together, even those of seeming minor affect. Be inspired by the work. Be encouraged by the harmonious relationships formed and developed at the table of spiritual leadership. Be optimistic at every turn, intersection and detour of Spirit's divine trajectory toward greater and greater blessings—some of which are unfolding even amid seeming delays, facades of chaos and vague misunderstandings. Trust that you have been called to serve. With trust, and the awareness that your consciousness matters, you will be able to own your yes, to a seat at the table. Dear friend own your yes. Own your YES!

Great Lessons Build Trust

In our ministry, when we were in our five-year search for our church home there came a time when frustrations were high and morale on the board and in the congregation was low. So, the board and I went on our annual retreat with the intention to pray for an entire weekend and come back with the location of a property given to us by Spirit. We rented a van and went to a retreat center where for three days we visualized, prayed, and affirmed that we would be guided to the location of our church home. On the third day we received a response that none of us could deny as we all received it at the same time, "Take care of what you already have." Well, as answered prayer goes, we were somewhat disappointed. We wanted to be able to go back to the congregation and say Spirit gave us an address and we know exactly where our new church home is located.

On the five-hour drive home from the retreat center we set about trying to clearly figure out what the message meant. We wondered how we would face the congregation. We knew they would be anxious to know the result of three full days of collective, focused prayer.

The clarity came when we walked into the leased store front space where we had our bookstore and administrative office. We immediately noticed that the carpet was torn in several places, that there was a stain on the ceiling from a leak in the roof, that one of the faucets in the kitchen area was leaking and our classroom area needed painting. We all knew what the message meant after seeing our facility with fresh eyes. We realized that we had been so busy looking for a new place that we had neglected to care for the current space. And, as disappointed as we were we decided to follow the guidance we received: "Take care of what you already have." We felt as if Spirit was saying that we would be in this space a little longer so clean it up and enjoy until the location of our new spiritual home would be revealed.

We immediately collected estimates for the work that needed to be done and submitted them to the landlord of the space we were leasing. He referred us back to our lease that said we were responsible for repairs made on the inside. He had repaired the leaky roof the year before and said, "It's up to you folks if you want to do repairs and renovations on the inside." Now, the estimates of what we wanted to do came to just over five thousand dollars, and according to our by-laws at the time we needed congregational approval to spend the funds. We decided to call a congregational meeting to first tell them of

e from Spirit, "Take care of what you already have" was
 us because the property that we purchased was a five-acre
, and five acres of land with five hundred avocado trees
are. Once we became good stewards of the leased facility,
strated the consciousness, willingness and readiness to be
 over a property that was larger and more beautiful than
e had viewed in our five-year search.

of the stories I enjoy telling again and again as my personal
e of the great lessons that started me thinking that to be
has great power and subsequent blessings. However, we
earn from the lessons we thought we'd mastered.

 finding our property, little did we know Spirit had an even
 for the board just ahead. We would have to go through
ivities that we were unfamiliar with from zoning, permits,
 the demonstration of funds to complete the purchase
y. However, we went into the process strong in our faith
Spirit guided us to our property, and because we had
 our willingness and readiness to own it, surely God would
gh the work required to possess it.

ck, I am absolutely persuaded that the only way to enter into
new building, entering into a renovation and construction
 the board functioning in unity and with one accord.

ommitted ourselves to prayer. Having experienced what
 do through us, and realizing we had a task ahead that we
 of the realm of our knowledge and expertise—at least on
realm. We were now "savvy" enough to know that we could
 to guide us through the uncharted road ahead.

 we would have to engage attorneys, architects, contractors,
nty enforcement officials, fundraising consultants all while
congregation engaged, excited and informed. So, we decided
 often, together as a board. We had seen and felt the power of
we wanted more.

the result of three days of prayer regarding the location of our spiritual home, and to gain approval to spend the necessary funds to renovate our leased space.

At first, the meeting did not go as smoothly as we had hoped. There were a few who questioned the result of our prayer. They wanted to know why Spirit had not given us something more concrete—like and address. Why in their opinion hadn't God answered our prayers? Next, the resistance came to putting money into a property that we were leasing. The thinking of those few at the time was *why not keep looking for our property instead of using money to renovate something we don't even own.*

Here is where I realized the value of how we arrived at what was ours to do as a board. In a moment of pure synergy and clarity, the board stood united in our position before the congregation because we arrived at the answer through prayer. We were convinced it was Spirit's message for us and for that reason we asked the congregation to join us and trust that we were operating on divine guidance. They did. We painted, installed new carpet, repaired the faucets, replaced tiles and with congregational help it ended up costing less than we expected.

Within thirty days of a "Yes" vote by the congregation, the property we eventually purchased "fell into our lap."

A few days after the congregational meeting, my assistant came into my office. "There's a realtor on the phone and he said he wants you and the board to come see a property immediately," she said.

Well, in retrospect I look back and say shame on me, for my response was, "Take his name and number and I'll get back to him. Since we've decided to fix this place up, we're not looking right now," I told her.

In a few minutes she came back, "He's very insistent. He said he has to get you to see the property as soon as possible."

I picked up the phone prepared to put him off. The voice on the other end said, "Rev. Manuel, I understand your church is looking for property to purchase."

"Yes, we've been looking for a while now, but we've decided to suspend looking for a while, we're renovating the facility we currently lease. It looks like we'll be here for a little while longer."

"Please come and see this property. A woman in your congregation has called me three times to inquire about this property and she asked me to call you. I don't think she's going to be satisfied until you see it," he said.

We set up two appointments that we did not keep. Several board members had scheduling conflicts, so we canceled the first two appointments. On the third try we set the appointment with the realtor

for a Thursday evening and carpooled from our bookstore location in two cars. When we pulled up to the gated address it was already dark, and we only saw trees and no building. As we pulled through the gate, drove through two acres of trees, we saw two buildings: a house and what looked to be a huge garage or a warehouse. We got out of our cars and all stood on the carport where the realtor was waiting for us. Standing on the carport, we all looked at each other and said in one voice "This is it."

"But you haven't seen the inside of the house or the warehouse yet," the realtor said.

Our board president spoke up, "We just know, this is it."

It dark, so we did not realize the full gift and beauty of the property until we came back on the following Saturday. The day time view revealed the beauty of the five hundred avocado trees that stretched over the five acres.

Then, we understood. We finally knew why it was so important to hear and follow the guidance we'd received on our retreat "Take care of what you already have." God was in the process of gifting us with a great

property that would require us to be good about to receive.

God doesn't test us but does prepare us f that we are ready to receive more—and sor "His master replied, 'Well done, good and faithful with a few things; I will put you in and share your master's happiness!'" (Matt

This story is filled with many lessons tha the process. We looked at how we arrived Quite frankly, I am convinced that if we ha to put money into our leased facility rathe purchase of our new property, there might board and a little negativity toward the bo; even suggest such a thing. But because we what Spirit had revealed to all of us, we we the congregants thought was "not the best

We learned as a board that answers to ou we receive may not always make good rati understanding. But if it is from Spirit, anc guidance we are willing to stand for, togetl the process was an awareness of the value each other. Together we had focused on a an energy we knew we had tapped into. W of synergy.

We learned how good it felt to be with o difficult to present to the congregation. W great strength in trusting God together, as used to demonstrate truth to our commur

Our congregation learned that they can listen to Spirit and to subsequently follow include them in the process.

The gu appropri avocado needs lot we had d good stev any prope

This is reminder of one acc continued

After fir greater hu a series of site plans, of the prop that becau demonstra lead us thr

Looking purchasing project is w

So, we re prayer coul knew was o the materia rely on Spir

In the ou bankers, co keeping the to pray moi synergy anc

Trust More, Pray More

We were already praying in teams on the board. Each board member had an assigned prayer partner to pray with weekly for a month then, we would rotate prayer partners. Over the years that process evolved into the entire board praying together over the phone on a weekly basis. We continued our weekly board prayer for sixteen years, through the completion of my tenure there.

When we were entering the renovation and construction phase of our journey, our board meetings became longer so we decided to add breakfast, lunch or dinner according to the time set for the meeting. We would discuss items from our agenda while eating so as not to add too greatly to the length of the meeting. It was much later that we realized that the sharing of the meal was a great bonding time for us to care with and for each other.

At one of our regular board meetings, a board member came to the meeting with a heavy heart, for several personal challenges prevented her from being mentally present to the business affairs on the agenda. During the meal which we always have at the beginning of the meeting, we decided we would just let this member share and set aside the agenda until after the meal.

We learned something that day. Our agenda went a lot smoother after everyone had an opportunity to share a little bit more than what we were accustomed to doing when we just did a brief check in. The meal time before the meeting became a time of personal sharing, a time to care for each other through listening and offering prayer support. Yes, the total meeting time became longer by not working through the meal; however, the value and quality of the relationships we formed in the process made it worthwhile to us. We realized that when members are not fully mentally present to the meeting due to personal stuff going on in their lives, more disagreements, objections, and misunderstandings would come up that really had little to do with the affairs of the ministry and more to do with what is going on in their personal lives.

When there is an opportunity for releasing the personal stuff followed by genuine care and prayer support, disagreements in the meeting get resolved a lot easier. We stress the point that even Jesus needed prayer support and asked for it, so no one need feel embarrassed about the challenges going on in their personal lives.

"And they, continuing daily with one accord in the temple, and breaking bread from house to house, did eat their meat with gladness and singleness of heart," (Acts 2:46).

We do not judge each other for what is shared at the table. We listen from a place of genuine compassion and offer prayer support. While every meeting is not extended due to lots of personal sharing, we allow the space during the meal time just in case it is needed.

Let Disagreement Be an Ally

Please do not be misled, our board surely had disagreements—we just handled them differently than in former times. Disagreements can be very healthy for the sake of looking at other perspectives, inspiring creativity and allowing for discussion where everyone feels heard. When it's okay to disagree, everyone feels free to speak their mind; the difference is we know that in the end when we leave the boardroom table we shall leave in unity. The level of connection we establish at the table is not a superficial meeting to "do business." There is a genuine sense of love, acceptance and appreciation for every person at the table developed through the time we invest in our relationship. Working through disagreements and challenges can either create division or strengthen our connection with greater unity.

Disagreement can even be a gift if we grow from it. One thing that can help embrace disagreement as healthy and necessary is in discerning when it is in the best interest of the ministry, and for the sake of unity on the board, to approve an issue based on consensus versus majority. Wisdom is applied to know when consensus is the best approach toward an issue. When consensus is arrived at through a prayer for guidance, rather than coercion or force, we can position the discussion toward collective discernment. Add to this the honoring of the Code of Conduct[1]

---

1   Discussed in Chapter one. Ephesians 4:1-6

invoking a commitment to "lead a life worthy of the calling to which you have been called, with all humility and gentleness, with patience, bearing with one another in love, making every effort to maintain the unity of the Spirit in a bond of peace." The decision can be tested to hold up the mission, vision and values assuring that we have honored the big picture. Here we are positioned for a unanimous decision. Disagreement is a time to be fully present and allow the highest and best decision to be revealed.

We discovered there are times when it is best to put in some additional prayer time or simply get more information before approving an item on the agenda where there is less than complete agreement. We were willing to either revisit an issue at a later date or release it all together to allow unity and harmony at the table or if it was of no great threat to the well-being of the ministry to set the issue aside for a while.

On one occasion, I brought an opportunity to the board that seemed to be one possible answer to a prayer we had been working on together. When I presented it to the board, I was sure all would agree. Well it turned out that two members did not think it was such a great idea: four voted yes and two voted no. As I listened to the two express their reasons for a "no" vote I really did not hear what I thought was a reasonable objection. Charline of former days might have been tempted to drag out a long discussion to help the two see how this was really a good thing. After giving it a fair time for discussion, I withdrew the proposal. Why? Because I respect both members greatly as valuable members of the board, I respect their "call of Spirit" to serve on the board, and I am bound to "make every effort to maintain unity" on our board. I still believe it would have benefited the church in a minor way but not to a level that it was worth pushing through on a majority vote and possibly disturbing the peace. It was also an opportunity for me to model humility.

Working together to maintain a bond of peace will most certainly guarantee that there will be disagreements at the table. However, there is a great lesson to be learned: working through differences we learn to trust each other. Any disagreement can be an opportunity to build trust and mutual respect if we are willing to work through it with a commitment to maintain harmony. The greater value is not always in the *outcome*, but in the *process,* we experience to get to our desired intent.

When we trust those along whose side we serve and when that trust is reciprocated, the reward of working through disagreement ultimately reveals itself as greater faith, peace and harmony around the boardroom table.

Affirmation for Spiritual Key #3

Every condition and circumstance we face carries a divine purpose with a divine solution revealed through our trust in Spirit and our trust in each other.

3rd Spiritual Key: TRUST

1. Let the power of frequent, joint prayer be a relationship builder of trust, peace, harmony and a strengthener of the board's collective faith.

2. The vibration of trust, faith, peace and harmony combined is a powerful magnetic force of synergy with the potential to attract great blessings.

3. Practice allowing disagreements to be an ally, make them teachable moments. Remember, differences often reveal hidden gifts that evolve into divine solutions embedded in what we may have originally perceived as a disagreement.

- To strengthen one-on-one relationships among the members consider establishing partnerships through prayer. Have a standard format such as a mastermind prayer format or create your own. Consider one-on-one prayer partners that rotate every month or a weekly group by phone or video chat. Expect members to make the prayer time a priority and trust they will participate as their schedules will allow.

- Use the prayer time to affirm the highest and best wisdom for the board; the health, growth, and prosperity for the congregation; the ministry as a whole; hold in the light any particular project you may be working on; and if a member has prayer request, offer prayer support for them during the call as well.

- Celebrate together. Relationships on the board level grow as you work at it. Take some time to enjoy and have fun together. Find ways to celebrate each other, great appreciation can be felt even in the smallest gestures.

Discussion Starters for Board Bonding – Trust

1. Discuss your perception of the trust level among board members. Are there additional things that can be done to build on the current trust level?

2. Tell a positive story of how trust impacted an event, activity or experience either on the board level or the ministry overall.

3. Before coming on the board what level of trust did you have in members on the board and how has that changed for you?

4. What is your understanding of how the board praying together can contribute and benefit relationships on the board, and the board's overall effectiveness.

5. When does the board exhibit great moments of harmony or synergy?

Spiritual renewal and the outer expression of appreciation—both, support the intention of ongoing harmony at the table.

Chapter Four

Spiritual Renewal

VALUE

"Then, because so many people were coming and going that they
did not even have a chance to eat he said to them, 'Come with me by
yourselves to a quiet place and get some rest.'"

--*Mark 6:31(NIV)*

When I was called to serve the ministry in Miami, the congregation
had been meeting in a beautiful Jewish synagogue for the Sunday
Celebration for about five years. They had leased a store front location
for Monday through Saturday operations: office space, commercial
bookstore and one room for classes. Our Sunday arrangement afforded
me the opportunity to meet and subsequently get to know the Rabbi. He
had founded that Temple some twenty-five years before I arrived. Upon
realizing I was fresh out of seminary he took it upon himself to offer the
kind of wisdom that comes with time and endurance as a religious and
spiritual leader.

Within a few months of my arrival, the Rabbi invited me to lunch. I
was a bit nervous about the lunch as he was not only a successful and
well-loved leader; he was well versed in many subjects including some
knowledge of our denomination. He was also a man of tall, healthy
stature and that contributed to his great presence. When he spoke, he did

so with authority. Over our seven-year acquaintance, he said and taught me many things. Although I did not understand all of what he shared, at the time, some things I remember to this day and now have a better understanding. For example, one time when I was sharing with him a challenge we were having in our ministry he replied, *"You'll never please all the people in your congregation, and if you do, you're not doing your job."*

And then there was another time he was sharing with me how he planned to handle a challenge he was having at the Temple, and almost like a footnote to his description of the difficulty he said, *"It's an impossible work that we pour ourselves into and once you lose site that it's impossible, you're in trouble."*

Another thing he said that stuck with me was *"Take care of yourself and your family, at the end of the day, those are the people who will be there for you—or not."* While I understood this one, I found myself struggling to achieve the balance he spoke of and I knew the Rabbi had as well.

He worked long hours and bore the pressure and great responsibility for the success of a large congregation, a school, an absolutely gorgeous-well maintained synagogue, and a full staff. Of course, he had the daily pastoral and executive roles that come with being the leader of a demanding community and still found the time to maintain the love and support of his wife, children and grandchildren. In addition, he was very active in religious, community and civic organizations. On his vacation trips to Israel he often took members with him (not a true vacation). As founding Rabbi, he had an overall good relationship with his twelve-member board, (Yes, 12!) but I remember many times listening to challenges he faced working to maintain peace around the boardroom table.

He made his transition of a heart attack at the age of sixty. I think that is when I really understood more of what he had tried to pass on to me in the short time we had together, mostly with me just listening and learning from him.

Jesus knew, understood and practiced the idea of taking time for refreshment and renewal. *He said to them, "Come away to a deserted place all by yourselves and rest a while." For many were coming and going, and they had no leisure even to eat.* The disciples had been working long hours and there was no time to relax and nourish themselves. So, Jesus took them on a "retreat."

Jesus understood that those around him needed renewal time and modeled this important practice by taking a retreat with them. But he also took time alone for renewal as well. Before he began his ministry, he set the tone for self-care and spiritual renewal by taking forty days alone in the wilderness. He took shorter retreats, some on his own and others with three of his closest disciples. Jesus taught and modeled that there is a correlation between effectiveness and taking time to renew mind, body and spirit.

Renewal for Board Members

If we want our leaders to be effective in their area of service, we must demonstrate that we value them. After the "incident" between me and the board who left the church, one of the first things we did after establishing a new board was to set a retreat date for ourselves. It was a bonding time for us and a time to process what the ministry had been through over the preceding months. I had set it in my mind that my relationship with all subsequent boards would be a priority for me. I knew first-hand what it was like to try to minister to others when the board and minister were at odds—and I vowed never to be in that predicament again.

We took a weekend at a retreat center. We shared, prayed with and for each other, laughed and generally spent time getting to know each other. It was a good way to start the task ahead of us to rebuild the trust of the congregation after going through a difficult time. The retreat process evolved over the years but generally we shared, prayed with and for each other, had a time of visioning for the future of the ministry, plan, set goals and share in at least one fun activity.

If our retreat center was near another ministry, rather than rush back to our church for Sunday service, on several occasions we used that time to attend Sunday service at whatever New Thought ministry was in the area. What a great experience for us to attend a service together and enjoy the spiritual nourishment of another spiritual community and witness how they functioned.

I have to say that our retreat time came to be one of my favorite times with our board. During the interview process for board membership, we informed prospective candidates that the annual retreat was mandatory for board service. The time was always the same time every year to help everyone plan well in advance to attend. In over twenty years, there was only two occasions when a board member missed the retreat due to an emergency. I noticed that since we get so much done in a weekend in a harmonious way, that the board member absent from the retreat missed what felt like the equivalent of missing three or four regular board meetings plus the added bonding time. Our annual board retreat was important to the harmonious functioning of the board and opened the way for a clear direction and path for our work for the year ahead.

While time to step away from the ministry for renewal, rest and reenergizing is important for both board and spiritual leader, the board has a bit of an advantage: board members have a set limit to their term of service and the by-laws generally limit the number of consecutive terms in which a member can serve. So, there is a scheduled finite period for board service; after which the bylaws generally build in a mandatory one-year rest period.

In addition to having set term lengths and limits, we reconfigured the roles on the board each year. We realized that some roles are more demanding than others so to avoid burn-out of one person functioning in a high demand role, we changed officers every year. This change also gives board members an opportunity to stretch and grow in areas where they have little or no experience. Board service is work. Honoring time for renewal through scheduled board retreats as well as individual participation in classes and workshops helped board members to remain in an overall attitude toward positive and willing service to the ministry. Board service should allow board members to stretch beyond their perceived capabilities in preparation for larger assignments from Spirit—in their personal lives as well as in board service.

Planning a Successful Board Retreat

Purpose. Assign some specific intentions behind the decision to "go apart for a while." Clear objectives will set the retreat as more than "just" time away. With substance to the agenda, the board members are

positioned for a positive experience and set the tone for achieving something of value for the ministry.

In a discussion with the board, discern what board members feel they want and need. There may be a desire to delve into subjects and topics at a deeper level beyond the limited time allotted in the average board meeting. Get board member input to any topics they believe will be helpful and substantive. If you've done a self-assessment questionnaire, the retreat is a great time to go over the results allowing time to discuss. This may also be a good time to review basic roles and responsibilities, share in some creative visualizing and brainstorming, open-up dialogue on issues that the board doesn't get to communicate on, but that may affect the ministry. Remember, whatever you do, the overarching goal is to lift-up the mission, vision and values and to support the ministries overall health, growth and prosperity. A bit of fun can also be uplifting for the board members so build some time for it into the agenda.

Venue: For the most part, the optimal environment for a board retreat is to get away from the building. Have a few days away if possible. At least every two years or so, strive to have the annual retreat off-site. Many retreat centers (some in your area) will work with boards on price, food and meeting rooms making it reasonable for a two or three-day getaway. If a retreat center does not work, then a hotel with meeting rooms may. However, I would be mindful of the "temptations" in a hotel environment versus a retreat center. Generally, hotels have things that could be distractions away from time for prayerful, meditative practices. All this to say, the venue is important and should be factored in planning a successful retreat.

Getting away from the building will allow for a fresh look at things when the board returns. I was always amazed that after we returned to the building even just for a weekend of prayer, meditation and visioning, how we saw things differently. When we returned we had "new eyes" on the building and how things had been done. Yes, our sight, focus and attention had changed. Being away, being together, being prayerful made a difference - imagine that! Do not underestimate the importance of the venue to a successful retreat.

Of course, if the budget will not allow for going away, your current facilities can be transformed to meet your needs. But do plan ahead, if you are not positioned to get away one year, set a plan on the following year and with prayer and intention surely it will come to pass. Finally, if the church budget does not allow for the expense of a board retreat, funding the retreat can be a board project or perhaps each board member could agree to contribute personally to the expense.

Building Trust: Team-building exercises give board members an opportunity to get to know one another on a deeper level, and practice communication and connection skills. This is a great opportunity to build trust among the members.

Facilitation. If possible have a facilitator who is not a member of the board, if not for all of it then at least for a part of the retreat. This way all members of the board can be fully engaged in the activities and exercises. If you use someone in your congregation, be mindful of their exposure to topics and subjects that may be confidential. When the budget allows, have a facilitator who has expertise in conducting retreats and who is not a member.

Beginnings matter. Start the retreat with a flexible check-in schedule that will allow board members to unwind and settle into retreat mode. It is also a great time to have an extended prayer time to allow members to join in a heart-centered connection. A solid heart connection at the beginning of your retreat can set an inspirational tone for the entire retreat.

Specific take-a-ways. From the retreat experience, the board should have written goals toward which to strive, with timelines and assignments. The same is true for each individual board member. Allow time for each member to share the thoughts, feelings, and ideas they will carry forward from their experience.

Endings matter. Close the retreat on a high note. Fun and laughter qualify for this. I generally set aside the last hour as "fun time." An assigned member of the board will be the facilitator of some fun activity. This can be a time to be of one accord in laughter, joy and light-heartedness. Yes, board service can be fun!

Evaluation. Do an evaluation afterwards so as to prepare the next board retreat, workshop or development exercise with even greater success.

Renewal for Spiritual Leaders

While some spiritual leaders serve in a ministry for a short period of time, the reason notwithstanding, the ministry will function for its greater good if there is reason to believe that there will be some continuity and longevity in their tenure.

If the hiring of the spiritual leader is thought of as "temporary" in the mind of the leader, the board, and the congregation, the things that make for building trust, a bond of peace and harmony simply do not have fertile ground in which to grow. Congregations that have a high turnover of spiritual leadership can begin to function from an unconscious expectation of abandonment, and thereby limit their opportunity to attract and establish a sense of stability for the ministry.

If the board plans for stability of leadership, that is to say that a newly hired spiritual leader will indeed be around for a while, the area of spiritual renewal should be addressed in discussion during the interview process and made part of the spiritual leader's contract. Additionally, where the board can really help with the health and well-being of the spiritual leader is to support them in taking the time granted in their contract including vacation, spiritual renewal, time for professional development and when the time comes—a sabbatical.

One of the most important responsibilities of the board is to assure that the spiritual leader has all that will support them as a healthy functioning ministry leader. These supports mainly involve ensuring an adequate salary with benefits, materials, supplies, staff, and time away for rest, and renewal. Support also means encouragement, shared mutual respect and the latitude to lead toward living the mission and striving forward to the vision. When the spiritual leader's needs are met, the ministry has a necessary component for a healthy status as the two operate in tandem.

Spiritual renewal is separate and apart from vacation time. This renewal time can range from a few days every quarter, a week every six months, or a week or two annually. The idea is to devise a strategy and plan that will work best for the spiritual leader while assuring that the ministry needs are taken care of as well. It is wise that the board be proactive with regard to meeting the needs of the spiritual leader. A healthy spiritual leader will be one whose needs are met allowing them to focus their time, energy and attention on the affairs of the ministry. The board's care and concern for the spiritual leader's well-being is also a vote of confidence in the leader's love and commitment to the ministry—this is priceless!

After five years in ministry, the initial enthusiasm I had for ministry had begun to wane. Things had occurred in those first five years that seminary had not prepared me for. Yes, I still loved ministry, I still loved the spiritual community I felt, honored to be a part of. But something in me felt a bit off. My first two years of ministry I diligently took spiritual renewal time once a quarter, two weeks' vacation, and Mondays and Fridays I did not go into the ministry office, but took time to handle personal affairs, relax, have fun and enjoy time with family.

However, over time in my third year, little by little my discipline of quarterly renewal disappeared into the busyness of ministry. My vacation time, if not spent out of town would be interrupted by some "emergency," and two days out of the office had evolved into one day of working from home, and the other was spent catching up on my personal affairs, laundry and house cleaning.

When on separate occasions, two fellow ministers told me that after seven years in ministry I should take a sabbatical, I was intrigued. I knew that if something didn't change, I would continue on a path where I would soon become another statistic—either experiencing ill health, leaving my current ministry for another, or out of ministry completely.

Many studies on the life of those who serve as clergy reveal that burnout statistics are high. The main reason recited is that spiritual leaders put in long hours. The great demands and high expectations that spiritual leaders face can carry with it a great deal of stress. Time for self-care, renewal and rest are a must.

The time, energy and effort a spiritual leader expends in ministry work is underestimated by the average congregant. Like the Rabbi said, "We'll never please all the people, nor is the job ever completely done." The work of a spiritual leader is subject to the events in the lives of others which effectively means, he or she is "on call" all the time. Yes, many tasks can and are delegated; however, to reference part of a familiar adage, *the buck stops with the leader.*

One of the things I have heard many times from first time volunteers in our ministry is how surprised they are that there is so much work involved in keeping the ministry going. And yes, new board members are most often surprised at the amount of work that goes into the minister's day to day, week to week, month to month business and administrative affairs of the ministry. In addition to the spiritual direction the minister has oversight of the pastoral needs of the members, as well as executive and administrative functions—all demanding of time and energy.

A good healthy dialogue around the boardroom table regarding renewal time for board members and spiritual leader is a sound discussion to have. With a good understanding of the value and importance of renewal, the discussion of a sabbatical for the spiritual

leader after five to seven years can be spent focused on the logistics for
the ministry rather than "if" the time off should be granted. Board
members have a built-in sabbatical since their terms have a specific
limit. However, for spiritual leaders the sabbatical must be scheduled
and intentionally planned.

A Sabbatical for the Spiritual Leader

A sabbatical can be a blessing for the spiritual leader and the ministry
if there is an understanding of its purpose, and the value to both,
followed up with planning and preparation for implementation. The
idea of a sabbatical for spiritual leaders has evolved from the Old
Testament statement in the allegory of the creation.

> "And on the seventh day God finished the work that he had
> done, and he rested on the seventh day from all the work that
> he had done. So, God blessed the seventh day and hallowed it,
> because on It God rested from all the work that he had done in
> creation," (Genesis 2:2-3 NRSV).

As this allegory goes, after God worked for six days on the great
spiritual work we call the creation, it says God took the seventh day off
to rest. God blessed the seventh day, called it a sacred time to rest from
the work God had done. And while we know that God never ceases
its vibrational energy of Being, or the divine love that binds everything
together functioning in perfect order, the seventh day simply marked a
time of completion.

The idea we infer behind this illustration is for those who function
in a leadership role in spiritual works, to take time to rest, renew and
re-energize from their work at prescribed intervals of completion. The
number seven is used extensively throughout the bible and generally
represents a time of completion. In the book of Leviticus, we read
that God spoke to Moses and gave instructions that there should be a
sabbatical year.

> "The LORD spoke to Moses on Mount Sinai, saying: Speak
> to the people of Israel and say to them: When you enter the

land that I am giving you, the land shall observe a Sabbath for the LORD. Six years you shall sow your field, and six years you shall prune your vineyard, and gather in their yield; but in the seventh year there shall be a Sabbath of complete rest for the land, a Sabbath for the LORD: you shall not sow your field or prune your vineyard. You shall not reap the aftergrowth of your harvest or gather the grapes of your unpruned vine: it shall be a year of complete rest for the land," (Leviticus 25:1-5 NRSV).

In the context of our discussion, I read this scripture symbolizing the "people of Israel" as the members of the ministry and the "land" as the spiritual leader. From the "land or spiritual leader" we reap the spiritual guidance, understanding of principles, divine laws and teachings so that we may appropriate the spiritual food that will nourish our souls. "The people" must give the land or "leader" an opportunity to rest in the seventh year so that fresh planting can be restarted in the following period for a good harvest in the future.

In the *Revealing Word*, Charles Fillmore discusses the Sabbath in a way that may further describe the idea of a sabbatical.

> The true Sabbath is that state of spiritual attainment where man ceases from all personal effort and all belief in his own works, and rests in the consciousness that "the Father abiding in me doeth his works" (John 14:10). When we understand the true spirit of the Sabbath, we cease following prescribed rules laid down by a church and open our mind to God's rest and peace. We rest from outer work, cease daily occupation, and give ourselves up to meditation or the study of things spiritual.

If we want our spiritual leaders to function in a way that they are at their best, willing and ready vessels for Spirit to work through them, then time for a sabbatical every seventh year is well worth it. The benefits for the ministry will be evident when the spiritual leader has been afforded the opportunity away, for greater time in prayer, inner work, spiritual study, professional development, rest and a bit of fun.

The specific logistics are best worked out for each particular spiritual leader and the ministry they serve. Sabbatical time is paid time spent away from the ministry and is in addition to vacation time. The board will need to develop a policy that allows this kind of renewal time for the spiritual leader, and if the ministry has paid associate ministers or spiritual leaders in key positions, consideration should be made for their sabbatical time as well.

When I prayed about the length of time for my first sabbatical, three months was my guidance. I proposed to the board taking two months in my seventh year and taking one month in the following year. That worked well for us. After the second year of having the one month off, the board noticed my renewed energy after a month off and decided that I would have available to me one month off each year in addition to my vacation time, and quarterly spiritual renewal time.

Before I took my first sabbatical the board and I took two years to prepare for it. On the board level we prayed about how to position the ministry to run smoothly in my extended absence. On the personal level I had to prepare myself, mentally, emotionally and financially[2] with a plan for what I wanted my sabbatical time to mean for me. One thing I learned about taking my precious sabbatical time was that to get the most from my time away, I needed to have an idea on what I needed and wanted for myself personally and professionally. Time apart from the congregation and the daily demands of ministry can be a great blessing for all concerned. However, it is also a demonstration of the value we project toward others by supporting and honoring their self-care needs.

Affirmation for Spiritual Key #4:
We value every member of our divinely appointed leadership team knowing individual health, growth and overall well-being benefits the full board and the ministry as a whole.

---

2 While a sabbatical is generally time off with full pay, funding for personal retreats, classes, studies and travel may need to come out of pocket. There are some foundations that offer grants for clergy sabbaticals that anyone can find with a little research on the internet.

4th Spiritual Key: VALUE

1. Create and implement ways to honor and demonstrate value for all board members, supporting their overall well-being.

2. Support and encourage opportunities for self-care, personal and professional growth for all members of the team.

3. Remember, Spirit needs every member of the team to be at their best, and that should include time apart for spiritual growth.

    • If the board is not already enjoying the benefits of an annual retreat, put it on the table for discussion. If you are already having regular board retreats, discuss what would give them greater value.

    • Have a discussion regarding how the ministry demonstrates its level of support and value for key leaders and volunteers.

    • Put a prayerfully drafted policy in place that will allow your ministry to honor spiritual renewal time for the spiritual leader and, when the time comes a plan for their sabbatical.

    • Schedule time for board spiritual enrichment, leadership development, or training on an annual basis. When possible take advantage of workshops if they become available in your area. Other opportunities may come through studying a book together, inviting consultants, guest speakers, or specialist to speak at your ministry.

    • Make provision to support the spiritual leader in his or her ongoing growth and development by funding their attendance at conferences, conventions, seminars, workshops, retreats or whatever the leader feels is best for their personal and professional growth and development, that is in alignment with an approved budget.

Discussion Starters for Board Bonding -Value

1. Discuss your understanding of the need for spiritual renewal for all board members.

2. Recall a class, workshop, seminar, vacation or retreat you have taken that left you with a sense of renewal and refreshment. What specifically about the event contributed to making it a positive experience for you?

3. Discuss the "built-in" sabbatical or "term limits" that board members have and its importance.

4. Discuss your understanding of the value of the sabbatical for the minister/spiritual leader.

5. Discuss ways and methods to demonstrate the importance of self-care for all those in leadership roles throughout the ministry.

Responsibility for, and the accountability to, the entire board, can often times avert a crisis, or help the team rebound more quickly if a great challenge occurs.

Chapter Five

Good Treasurer, Bad Decision

RESPONSIBILITY

"Then one of the twelve, who was called Judas Iscariot, went to the chief priests and said, "What will you give me if I betray him to you?" They paid him thirty pieces of silver."

--Matthew 26:14-15 (NRSV)

Now, we all know that Judas is indeed the least liked of all the disciples for his "betrayal" of Jesus. While I know Judas is a controversial figure I'd like to offer an alternative perspective of Judas's motive and subsequent decision to turn Jesus over into the hands of those who sought to kill him. Additionally, I will offer a fictitious outcome of Judas' actions that may help us uncover a lesson in spiritual leadership for current times. Consider that Judas' story (with a bit of fictitious interjection) is one from which we can extract a teachable moment to benefit boards of trustees today.

When we read through the scriptures, history records Judas as "the one who betrayed Jesus" or "traitor" or, as in one story where he is referred to as a "thief." In today's culture and understanding the name Judas has evolved to reference anyone who we believe to be a traitor. Who among us would want to be known and remembered for a single act or event in our lives?

In defense of Judas, I introduce a term that was not around in Judas' day that may be relevant to how he is referred to. The term is "Monday morning quarterbacking," it means to criticize or pass judgment from a position and view, after the fact. The bible was written long after Judas was identified as Jesus' betrayer. So the writer would tell Judas' story from the lens of the one event that made him "infamous." Because the outcome is so devastating and contemptible, the writer judged all Judas' previous acts and actions according to the results of the final outcome—one single event. For example, notice the story in the Gospel of John chapter twelve.

> "Then took Mary a pound of ointment of spikenard, very costly, and anointed the feet of Jesus, and wiped his feet with her hair: and the house was filled with the odour of the ointment. Then saith one of his disciples, Judas Iscariot, Simon's son, which should betray him, Why was not this ointment sold for three hundred pence, and given to the poor? This he said, not that he cared for the poor; but because he was a thief, and had the bag, and bare that was put therein," (John 12:3-6).

Consider this scripture minus the "commentary" regarding Judas and let us "pretend" we do not know Judas' fate. The scripture would read as follows:

> Then took Mary a pound of ointment of spikenard, very costly, and anointed the feet of Jesus, and wiped his feet with her hair: and the house was filled with the odour of the ointment. Then saith one of his disciples, Judas Iscariot, Simon's son, Why was not this ointment sold for three hundred pence, and given to the poor? Because he had the (money) bag.

Minus the negative remarks toward Judas' character, this scripture conveys that Judas was simply doing what good "keepers of the funds" do. He questioned if he thought there might be a missed opportunity to collect funds for the ministry, he questioned if those funds could have been used in an area that would further support the mission. Yes, he carried the bag of funds—treasurers usually do have some authority over keeping the funds—someone has to.

But because the writers knew the outcome of Judas' fate, it was easy to Monday morning quarterback and espouse *surely, he must have been a thief then, because later he became known as a traitor who sold Jesus out for money. Surely, he could not have been concerned about the mission of helping the poor then, because later he betrayed the mission by betraying Jesus. Because he had the opportunity as the one who collected and carried the money bag, surely, he must have stolen money then, because later he took money from Jesus' enemies.*

The question is "Does the end, clarify or reveal the details of the means?" There may be times when we can predict with "some" accuracy certain behaviors before they happen. However, if we are only looking through the lens of the end, pieces of the middle details cannot always be accounted for. So, the writers, put together their best guess of what happened, based on their understanding of the end. If it were possible to figure out the middle based on the end, just think, with the technology and forensic methods we have today, we would have no unsolved crime cases, yet we do.

When we consider that Jesus called Judas to discipleship along with the others and subsequently appointed Judas as treasurer, surely Jesus was following his own divine guidance. Either Jesus misjudged Judas' character, and made an unwise decision in calling Judas to discipleship, or afterwards Judas's heart changed toward greed, and Jesus failed to confront him or, Judas had what he thought was a creative idea to what he perceived as a money problem. All in all, at some point, Jesus must have believed that Judas would indeed make a good disciple and chose to test him or promote him to treasurer.

As treasurer, Judas was the keeper of the funds for Jesus's ministry. He gathered and disbursed whatever monies needed for Jesus, the disciples and probably a rather large entourage to travel from town to town doing the work of Spirit. Just as treasurers do today, Judas kept an eye on the expenditures for questionable items for the sake of good stewardship.

Could it be that Judas cared about having the resources needed to help Jesus' message reach many, and subsequently found himself lured into the temptations of materialism? Or could he have taken his role as treasurer very serious, too serious and in the process lost sight of the true goal? Judas was not the first, nor the last to be blinded by what may have appeared to be the light of righteousness, only to discover it was an intense glare of obsessive passion which most always leads to "bad" decisions.

When the Disciples Did Not Act with One Accord

Obviously when Judas accepted thirty pieces of silver to turn Jesus over to those who sought to kill him, the disciples were not functioning with one accord. When the spiritual team is not connected, bound together in a unity of purpose, or guided to maintain peace and harmony, focus toward the common good gets betrayed for false gain.

The idea of everything we've talked about in this book so far is about building a consciousness of oneness among the board members. It is not to suggest that we act with one accord on special occasions or for specific projects. The power of being with one accord is revealed as an overall attitude toward board service. If the disciples had been close—that is responsible for, and accountable to each other, someone on the team should have noticed Judas' change. Working as a team, someone would have seen Judas' focus toward obsession about money, his fear around money, his secrecy—something. Why didn't one, two, three or all the disciples notice his behavior building up to his "bad" decision and do an intervention?

Let me just say I'm not trying to circumvent Jesus's crucifixion, nor am I challenging the human need to cross out personality and all error thoughts from consciousness. All is in divine order and Spirit will reveal the lessons to attain and demonstrate eternal life one way or another. But

I am looking at the people who were around Jesus as his leadership team and asking why didn't Judas' plan get derailed or interrupted by other members on the team?

On a spiritual team working together with one accord, for the common good, someone would have noticed Judas' behavior and pulled him aside to talk him through whatever he was going through.

When we serve on a board of trustees we become part of a "team" and that may even mean speaking to another member who is shifting focus away from our unity of purpose and the effort to serve for the greater good.

The idea of being with one accord sounds good as a theory. That's all it is until it is brought to life by the work and effort of the members of the team. To maintain a position of unity, the members on the team must be willing to take responsibility for a unified position and be accountable to each other in attitude and actions.

I'm not talking about the quote we hear regarding "good men doing nothing," but rather the genuine care and support we share as members on God's team—going for the best that "we" can be. Divine love is a healing, prospering, comforting, forgiving, uplifting power that we have as a spiritual teaching. Board service will present opportunities to help every member grow in their use of the spiritual teachings we follow. If one member has a difficult time on the team, through the power of divine love, an offer of support is provided. And, if we are striving to use the spiritual keys in this book, we shall have the tools to operate with integrity, sincerity and compassion.

We recognize and understand that any member around the boardroom table is capable of making a poor choice, a "bad" decision. However, we also acknowledge our commitment to work toward a consciousness of unity and therefore we must be vigilant over our relationships. In this way we will be alert to another member who displays a signal for help, even if the signal is subtle.

Before my days in seminary, I was a church employee and had access to the following story. A long-time member and very successful business woman was voted on the board of trustees of the church. The minister at that time believed that she would be a good treasurer and the other board members agreed. She had proved herself to be very competent in financial matters as the founder and owner of a business with many employees, plus she was the church's strongest and most consistent tither. She had given generously to special projects in the church well over and beyond her tithes. From all accounts, she was great for the role of treasurer.

For a few years with this woman as the treasurer working harmoniously with the minister, the church prospered. If there was a shortfall in offerings she would on occasion, make up the difference needed to keep things going smoothly. But one day the minister went to cash his paycheck and it bounced. He went into the church office and began to look through the church checkbook and discovered several entries missing and check stubs not filled in. Upon meeting with the bank, it was determined that several checks totaling over eleven thousand dollars had been written to this woman's personal company and cashed by her.

The minister's disappointment was not just in the money that was taken, not just that it was a criminal act against the church, but also because he knew that she had been a good truth student, good member of the church, one of his biggest supporters since he arrived at the church. And—up to that point, she had been a really good board member and treasurer.

When he sat down with her, the minister revealed the financial situation he had discovered. She cried, she wept and begged for forgiveness. She admitted that she wanted to come to him to talk about it but was too embarrassed to approach him. She said how much she loved the church but when her business faced a big financial setback, her only known solution was to borrow the funds from the church and pay the money back before anyone would find out.

While he did not blame himself, the minister found himself disappointed not just in the treasurer but disappointed in himself also. He had noticed that something was going on with this woman and failed to take the time to find out what was troubling her. He believed that had he taken the time to lend his support that a different solution could have been achieved before this trusted board member committed an act of theft. I know that the woman left the church but do not know if the funds were ever repaid. I know the minister mourned the loss of what he believed to be a good member of the church, and for several years a good trustee on the board—who made a very unwise decision.

We all know good people who have made poor choices. However, let us also know that sometimes poor choices can be interrupted by well-meaning friends, associates or spiritual partners who recognize that even a good heart can be tempted under stressful circumstances.

I venture to say that all treasurers, all trustees want the best for the overall ministry. Yet, when certain personal issues rise to a level of high anxiety, many of us are ripe for zealous actions of the not so wise persuasion. Problems involving money just happens to be one of those "high anxiety" type issues that have led many to veer off the path of wise decision making. Even in the loving, spiritual environment of ministry some "bad" decisions have been made by trustees and spiritual leaders who may have chosen differently if someone close to them had offered a listening ear, a compassionate heart, wise counsel and a prayer.

Back to Judas as Treasurer

The story of Judas is a good one to use as it is well known for the outcome but also it brings up the subject of money. Ministries needed money back in Jesus' day just as they do today. As treasurer, Judas might well have had some concerns over the offerings. So, take an imaginary journey with me into a conversation that treasurer, Judas could have had with Jesus, spiritual leader.

Again, this is my dramatization of a brief encounter that Jesus and Judas "might" have had six months before Judas took matters into his own hands.

Judas: "Teacher, the offerings have been getting lower and lower since I last spoke with you on the finances. Soon there will not be enough money to keep things going."

Jesus: "Judge not according to the appearance, but judge righteous judgment," (John 7:24).

Judas: "You're a great spiritual teacher but I don't think you understand how much money it takes to feed all the disciples, the women and children. Plus, the material for clothing and the supplies has gone up recently, not to mention the expensive oils and incense you enjoy. Jesus, we need money and you don't seem to be concerned, I'm worried we'll run out of money and soon."

Jesus: "Do not worry, saying, 'What shall we eat?' or 'What shall we drink?' or 'What shall we wear?' For your heavenly Father knows that you need all these things. But seek first the kingdom of God and His righteousness, and all these things shall be added to you," (Matthew 6:31-33 NKJV).

Judas: "I just think we can do more to either... cut back on expenses or, increase the offerings—maybe take up a second offering, or get a large sum of funds that will last us until things improve. In fact, I don't want to share any details but I'm working on a deal right now that may bring in so much money we won't have to worry about money for a long time."

Jesus: "Judas, where is your faith?"

Judas: "I have faith, I do. I've been listening to all the stuff you say, and I get it. But I just think that if we..."

Jesus: "If you know these things, blessed are you if you do them," (John 13:17 NKJV).

Judas: "Okay, but just hear me out. It may sound a little bizarre at first but I'm talking a major deal here. So, they want to kill you, you've been telling us for months now about your death, but it doesn't have to be that way. See, I say we capitalize on their desire to kill you, I think they'll pay a lot of silver to get their hands on you."

Jesus: "The Son of Man is about to be betrayed into the hands of men," (Matthew 17:22 NKJV).

Judas: "No, no, it's not like that at all. See I would negotiate a sum that would be enough to set us in a sound position. We could leave this region immediately and return in a year or so, things would be different then. All you have to do is use your powers to break free from them. They might try to rough you up a bit, but…I mean all this stuff you've been teaching us won't it work for you as well? Won't your Father save you from the hands of those who attempt to interfere with the work He put you here to do?"

Jesus: "No one can serve two masters; for either he will hate the one and love the other, or else he will be loyal to the one and despise the other. You cannot serve God and mammon," (Matthew 6:24 NKJV).

Judas: "Yeah, you told us that before. But when you multiplied the two fish and five loaves and fed five thousand, plus women and children, I got to thinking you could do so much more if we had more money. See here's my plan, if they offer me let's say ten pieces of silver, I'll get them up to at least twenty. Who knows they might be willing to go even higher, if they do, I'd jump at it. With that kind of money, the offerings we get from the people would just be icing on the cake. Don't you see? I'm talking thousands[3] of dollars here, ten thousand maybe more. The money would put you in a position where the world would have to take notice. Isn't that what you want?"

Jesus: "For what profit is it to a man if he gains the whole world, and loses his own soul? Or what will a man give in exchange for his soul? For the Son of Man will come in the glory of His Father with His angels, and then He will reward each according to his works," (Matthew 16:26-27 NKJV).

---

3   While there is no way to determine the value of thirty pieces of silver from Jesus' time to the current day, if we base our guess according to purchasing power, we shall speculate its current value to be at least into the thousands of dollars.

At that moment the other disciples began to gather for the evening meal. Jesus moves in close to Judas and takes both his hands into his and looks into his eyes.

Jesus: "Every kingdom divided against itself is brought to desolation, and every city or house divided against itself will not stand," (Matthew 12:25 NKJV).

Judas: "I alone have carried the burden of the money bag for too long, and no one else seems to care. If I don't do something, we won't have the funds we need to continue. I knew they wouldn't understand, (glancing briefly in the direction of Peter and John who were just taking a seat at the table), not once have they offered to stay afterwards and count the offering or help me get supplies. I thought surely you would appreciate the work I am doing to assure that we have the money we need to keep things going."

Their conversation ends as the other disciples yell out "Teacher, come bless the meal, we're hungry."

Okay maybe a little too dramatic but you get the idea. Here is a trustee who is frustrated while trying to fulfill what he believes is his role in the ministry.

I realize this creative allegorical dramatization gives Judas a benefit that history has not. I'm not trying to rewrite history nor am I asking you, the reader, to believe this dramatization. Consider if you will that there may have been a moment in time when Judas, acting in his duties as trustee and treasurer, under Jesus' appointment, was indeed a good treasurer and subsequently made a "bad" decision.

If Judas took the thirty pieces of silver for personal gain and selfish greed alone he would not have gone to the chief priests to give the money back when he saw what was happening to Jesus. When they would not take the silver back, his grief was too much to bear and he took his own life. Surely Judas believed Jesus would use his "power" to get himself free. Even those present at the crucifixion that had only a glimpse of Jesus teachings believed Jesus would "save" himself. "And the people stood beholding. And the rulers also with them derided him, saying, He saved others; let him save himself, if he be Christ, the chosen of God," (Luke 23:35).

The point I make is that before Judas accepted the thirty pieces of silver, he had every reason to believe that Jesus would *not* be crucified. Would he have used all or some of the thirty pieces of silver for personal benefit? Who knows, but his conscience seemed to suggest that his misguided actions may have been more error in judgment than absolute greed for personal gain.

One of the main functions of the board of trustees is to assure that the ministry has the funds needed to function and grow, all while fulfilling the mission. Boards oversee that all assets are managed under good stewardship.

However, there can be times when the offering is not at the level we need to meet the expenses of the ministry, or the additional funds may not be readily available to fund new programs and projects that will allow for the fulfillment of the mission. So, from the standpoint of being a good trustee, measures must be taken as a means of assuring the ministry has the funds needed.

One of the things new board members often find eye opening is the amount of funds it takes to operate a ministry and keep it growing. We had a few board members over the years in our ministry who once they began serving on the board discovered that they did not want the accountability of being involved with the finances; it was a greater responsibility than they had imagined.

Once it is realized that it takes funds to operate the ministry, the trustees who embrace the roles and responsibilities take it seriously. And it can happen that in an effort to assure that the funds for the ministry are available, fear can arise in the heart of board members and spiritual leader alike.

So, in writing this book on being with one accord in board service, I cannot leave out a discussion on ministry finance and in the next chapter I will say more on this. But for now, I have to say that when I hear of a "crises" around the boardroom table of a spiritual community, I listen very carefully for somehow money or a financial issue is usually somewhere in the mix. Let's face it while money is *not* the root of all evil, it is often used as a good excuse to awaken unresolved issues or it can become a catalyst for buried thoughts, feelings and emotions to rise to be dealt with among board members and between spiritual leader and the board as a whole.

In my own "board incident" years ago, this was true. What I did not reveal in the telling of "my side" of the story is that "one" of the issues that the board at that time had with me did center around a difference of understanding on a money issue. An unresolved issue we had regarding my salary and contractually agree upon performance bonus became a catalyst and a spark for a fire that over several months grew until it was out of control. By the time they attempted to fire me, the issue of unpaid funds due to me was way down on their "list" of complaints and reasons I should be fired, but the unresolved money issue opened the door.

Money is often factored in making decisions, even when it is not the real issue or as relevant as some would have us believe. Again, I say money is not the root of all evil, but it sure does find itself hidden secretly within many a crisis situation.

Some things are priceless, and to learn what those things are is part of life's journey. Those who misplace money front and center of an issue where it should be considered last, least or maybe even not at all may find themselves facing consequences that are unpleasant, devastating or even tragic. This is a lesson some board members and spiritual leaders must learn, and quite frankly it's not usually an easy lesson.

A Joint Responsibility

One of the board's key responsibilities is good stewardship over the ministry funds. Stewardship is a responsibility that should honor

Thaddaeus: "So where do we go from here?"

James, son of Alphaeus: "We must remember all that our teacher told us, or else…or else what did it all mean? Somehow, we've got to accept it and figure out what comes next."

All our relationships challenge us with a dual obligation—responsibility and accountability. We are to own responsibility for our actions and then be accountable for the consequences of those actions. In a team centered relationship, every member on the team is expected to give their best and should expect others to do the same. When it appears that a teammate has fallen away from his or her best, we have the responsibility to be accountable *for the sake of* the individual member and the team, to lend support, in the name of getting the team back to a state of functioning from its best self. On a team, the actions of one individual can affect the entire team, so responsibility and accountability is an invisible cord that binds the members together.

Let Love be the Starting Place Toward Reconciliation

When strong differences emerge, on the board, the last thing to be brought into question should be each person's love for the ministry. If we have been intentional during the board selection process, and implemented the spiritual keys in this book, love for the ministry will have demonstrated itself.

Everyone around the boardroom table makes a great sacrifice of their personal time to have a seat at the table. It is love that compels each member to give generously of themselves. "As God's chosen ones, holy and beloved, clothe yourselves with compassion, kindness, humility, meekness, and patience. Bear with one another and, if anyone has a complaint against another, forgive each other; just as the Lord has forgiven you, so you also must forgive. Above all, clothe yourselves with love, which binds everything together in perfect harmony. And let the peace of Christ rule in your hearts, to which indeed you were called in the one body. And be thankful," (Colossians 3:12-15 NRSV).

Love can be a great starting point toward establishing, maintaining and striving for harmony. Let it be the common denominator of those who by giving of their time, talent, and treasure have earned a seat at the boardroom table.

Charles Fillmore says in *Keep a True Lent,*

> There is a distinction between love of the divine type, exercised by divine man, and love of the human type, exercised by the mortal man. It requires discriminating judgment to distinguish between human and divine love. All love is divine in its origin, but in passing through the prism of man's mind it is apparently broken into many colors. Yet, like the ray of white light, it ever remains pure. It is within man's province to make its manifestation in his life just as pure as its origin. This too requires painstaking discrimination and good judgment. We learn by experience that love must be directed by wisdom. If we give up blindly to the impulses suggested by human love, we shall suffer many downfalls.

In times of disagreement let us not question each other's love for the ministry, but rather count on it. We can rely on the power of divine love to heal and restore a broken connection. Another's love may be showing up in a very different way from our own, but is just as real through their unique prism of consciousness. With love for the ministry as a foundation, our work together will be to draw forth the wisdom of Spirit. When divine love and the wisdom of Spirit meet in the middle of a challenge, we position ourselves for the restoration of peace.

If each member at the table has a sincere desire for love and wisdom to guide the discussions and subsequent decisions made, the collective faith of the board will be strengthened. Ask in prayer for divine guidance and prepare to let the decision be directed by the truth principles at the core of the ministry. We may be guided to seek help from other ministry leaders, consultants, finance or legal specialists. The words attributed to

Jesus are sound advice "Ask, and it will be given to you; seek, and you will find; knock, and it will be opened to you," (Matthew 7:7 NKJV).

Affirmation for Spiritual Key #5:

We take shared responsibility along with individual and collective accountability for the work that is ours to do on behalf of our ministry.

5th Spiritual Key: RESPONSIBILITY

1. Own the idea that Spirit has assembled and equipped a carefully crafted team to accept spiritual leadership as a divine appointment.

2. All board members bear responsibility and share in accountability—to Spirit, self and to fellow spiritual partners who serve at the boardroom table.

3. The board is a fiduciary of the church's resources and champions for the church's mission, vision and values.

   • Honor and respect the divine appointment of each member of the board. Respect the team by being responsible for individual action and accountable to other members on the board to help maintain a unified position for the board as a whole.

   • If there is occasion when a member's action infer a challenge in their personal life or with something regarding the affairs of the ministry, error on the side of caution by making a sincere inquiry into their well-being. The offer of a listening ear is usually not offensive, especially when it's made from genuine concern and received by one who really needs it.

   • Have a discussion with fellow board members regarding the level of responsibility attributed to the board for the actions of other board members—legally, financially and practically. Have a discussion also regarding accountability and the expectations of each person giving their conscious best as spiritual partners, working toward a common overall goal for the purpose assigned to God's carefully crafted team.

Discussion Starters for Board Bonding -Responsibility

1. Discuss your understanding of how good people can some times make a "bad" decision.

2. If, and only if you feel comfortable in sharing, tell of a time when you made a "bad" decision (This can be personal or business). What did you learn from the experience?

3. What are some of the ways that we can make amends when a "bad" decision is involved?

4. What can board members do to support each other in fulfilling the roles and responsibilities in board affairs?

5. What can board members do to assure that board officers and the minister/spiritual leader get the support they need to function at their best?

When the world of the Spirit in which we live by divine law, and the material world in which we must deal with business entities, banks, government requirements and taxes collide at the boardroom table, a shift in consciousness prompting a financial stimulus—mind and material, may be in order.

Chapter Six

When an Increase in Funds is Needed

AGREEMENT

"So great fear came upon all the church and upon all who heard
these things. And through the hands of the apostles many signs and
wonders were done among the people. And they were all with
one accord in Solomon's Porch."

--Acts 5:11-12 NKJV

At no greater time is it extremely important for the board members and
the spiritual leader to be with one accord than when the ministry finds
itself in the position of consciously desiring to increase available funds.
An article published in the November 1908 issue of Unity Magazine[4] had
this to report on this topic:

> A union of many minds on a good thought is like a company of
> men lifting a weight by all exerting themselves at the same time.
> They do not stop to argue or question. When the "heave ho!" is
> given they lift with one accord, and up goes the burden.

The ministry leadership has an incredible responsibility in that we
look to Spirit as our Source, follow the ways of faith, wisdom and love in
all our interactions and administrative operations. However, there are

---

certain material realm regulations and laws to be followed in order to get things done that allow the ministry to function, grow and prosper.

If our ministry is indeed fulfilling a mission that is Spirit guided, we shall have opportunities to work and grow through, times of change, transition and expansion. Just as life is cyclical, so will it be that our ministry shall be subject to opportunities to endure, shift, stretch and broaden our ministry's potential. "To everything there is a season, and a time to every purpose under the heaven..." (Ecclesiastes 3:1). Just as we have seasons in our personal lives, so too does the ministry face seasons with recurrent possibilities for spiritual evolution, *the unfolding of the Spirit of God into expression.*[5] So let us admit that there may be times in the process of growth, evolution and expansion that the board, acting on behalf of the ministry must be conscious and mindful to balance the visible demonstration of funds and the invisible resources available through faith in God as our source.

For many years (seventeen to be exact), before I arrived at the church in Miami, and for several years more, we did not have our own facility, meeting place and spiritual home. The church moved frequently from rented space to rented space until the minister who preceded me contracted meeting space for the Sunday Celebration at a beautiful synagogue. When I arrived, they were already comfortable with the synagogue as their Sunday meeting place. The congregation ended up meeting in that Temple for eighteen years before we moved to the five-acre avocado grove the ministry purchased and subsequently paid-off during my tenure.

Why did it take so long one might ask? So, let me backtrack just a bit. At the point when I was hired the ministry had for seventeen years become accustomed to moving around, they had accepted the old "church in a box" position and had become quite comfortable with it. Even after the synagogue was established as the regular Sunday meeting place, we still moved in on Sunday mornings and out on Sunday afternoons. Although we had a good relationship with the Rabbi and the Jewish congregation, there were some Sundays when we had to meet somewhere else because the synagogue needed or wanted to use their sanctuary.

---

5   Keep a True Lent, Charles Fillmore, published by Unity School of Christianity.

Most times we had advance notice, a few times a year we did not.

Three months into my tenure, after experiencing: a need to move our Sunday service with a one-week notice, an increase in the rent we paid, and an early Monday morning phone call from the synagogue administrator that started out "Rev. Manuel, your children moved some of the toys belonging to our children when they met yesterday in the youth building, this is unacceptable," I was ready for us to find our own home.

So, one Sunday I said to the congregation "We need our own space." Well, after the service ninety-five percent of the people who came through the exit line rendered comments like, "We don't need our own space, we're happy here," "We don't have money to buy a new building," or "This location is perfect, if you move the church I won't be coming here anymore."

As the new kid on the block, I could see a need that was not obvious to those who had become comfortable with things the way they were. I do admit that the synagogue had everything we thought we wanted and needed: a 350-seat sanctuary with beautifully stained-glass windows, well-equipped with lighting and sound systems, a huge fellowship area with kitchen, a ballroom with a full commercial kitchen, plenty of classrooms for the youth and reasonable amount of parking. Why would our congregation ever want to leave such a place?

Now, I know I mentioned "Monday morning quarterbacking" in the last chapter, so here it applies again. Looking back, I came to realize that I had not introduced the idea in the "best" way. (Again, I was three months out of seminary). The average congregant was happy meeting at the synagogue. The few who were "somewhat" open to the idea were,

- Those who did the "work" on Sunday mornings,
- Those who wanted to take classes during the week. The synagogue was not open to us other than on Sundays. (Although we were leasing a storefront property for office space, bookstore and classes it had limited parking available),

- The children who wanted to put their pictures and artwork on the walls and have their own materials and supplies for their enjoyment and use on Sundays,
- The Board who knew firsthand the financial cost, of renting two separate locations and the inconvenience of the logistics caused by maintaining both.

The concerns of the overwhelming majority became the topic of discussion in the fellowship area on Sundays. The good news that grew from my "blurting out" our need for our own space was that we, (the board and I) heard where the congregation stood. Few wanted to move from the comfort and beauty of the synagogue. However, a growing fear began to emerge as we, (I) had planted a seed in un-ready soil—the idea of property ownership. This newly introduced goal would require a greater demonstration of money and suddenly money was on everyone's mind.

While the board recognized the need for our own space, the idea brought up all kinds of disagreements regarding the "how to, and when" followed by that growing recognition that we (I) had not done any preparation work, "Where will the money come from?"

Because I had not sown the seed idea of owning our own property on good, (ready) soil, we were in for a series of great lessons. We spent the next five years searching, looking at properties, making unsuccessful offers, meeting with realtors, town meetings and hosting several prayer vigils. After finding the property it took an additional two-year process to work through five bank financing rejections, getting the property rezoned, getting site plans drawn and approved by county officials, acquiring the funds and taking possession of the property. It took seven years of work (lessons) to arrive at the time of completion. "What was sown on good soil, this is the one who hears the word and understands it, who indeed bears fruit" (Matthew 13:23).

The resistance we had within our own congregation out-pictured itself in the many obstacles and delays we faced. The disagreements on the board as to *if, when,* and *how* to purchase our own spiritual home, became a significant mountain to climb. The Unity Magazine quote from the beginning of this chapter speaks to two important tenets I have come to believe with regard to raising funds and working toward projects that require an increase of funds. First begin on ready soil. Second get a union of minds *before* exerting great energy then, lift *with one accord*.

> "Again I say unto you, That if two of you shall agree on earth as touching anything that they shall ask, it shall be done for them of my Father which is in heaven," (Matthew 18:19).

"Again," the verse starts. In other words, Jesus is saying something like, I've told you this before, but it bears repeating—it's that important. Before two or more ask, be with one accord; agree on earth, so that the "heavenly" solution or the divine answer and guidance can be revealed to a unified team. This is the power that reveals itself in the form of synergy. Agreement is a powerful energy from which we can achieve amazing things.

We had a cloud of resistance hanging over our heads from the overwhelming majority of the congregation who expressed great reluctance around leaving the safety, comfort and beauty of the synagogue. I had come to terms with an idea I had not considered: If we are comfortable and someone else bears the responsibility of providing that comfort, why would we want to leave that comfortable state of existence? So, we learned the lesson of preparation.

Also, there was the concern that centered around money. We heard many times during the process although phrased in many different ways "Where is the money coming from?" As the spiritual leader, I found new respect for Moses' plight leading the children of Israel out of Egypt, a reference my Rabbi friend reminded me of several times. "…and the people complained against Moses, and said, "Why *is* it you have brought us up out of Egypt, to kill us and our children and our livestock with thirst?" [4] So Moses cried out to the LORD, saying, "What shall I do with this people? They are almost ready to stone me!" (Exodus 17:3-4 NKJV).

The board and I knew we had a lot of work ahead of us, but we also knew that if we succeeded, the rewards would be worth it. So we learned the lesson of agreement. Along the way we discovered that there is great power in agreement. Energy is magnified. When we began to practice Jesus' instruction to "re-check" what we "agree" upon before we ask, things began to move, the consciousness began to shift—a little. Once we discovered the gift, being of one accord, we set in motion conditions by which Spirit could act according to a singleness of purpose.

After we worked out the details of our own disagreements on the board level, it was by the power of agreement that we were able to stand united in the face of many obstacles with a mighty strength to tolerate the criticism, complaints, and complications we faced on the journey to our "promised land." What I observed first hand: The board of trustees can promote a healthy prosperity consciousness for the ministry by functioning as a spiritual team, working spiritual law.

Over the years we were faced with many opportunities when we desired to raise funds. We discovered that our efforts were delayed when we ourselves were not all in agreement and had not prepared the congregational consciousness. We knew too that any major fundraising project should rest on solid prayer before engaging the "heave-ho." Once there was agreement between us, and our energy was synchronized, then "the Father which is in heaven," or "through divine law" we would receive the go forward signal by way of open doors and green lights.

Getting to Agreement

The path to agreement is often pursued through attempts to force ideas and opinions upon each other, sometimes in fierce debate or in arguments that plead our varying points of view. One of the ideals around moving through disagreement is to shift the collective energy to one of openness and possibility. Disagreement often allows us to shut down our interest in listening, engaging and participating in amicable resolutions.

Here we can use our faith centered belief in the power of prayer and rely on our spiritual practices to recalibrate the attitudes and altitude at the boardroom table. A centering prayer or extended meditation before we delve into discussions that may be contentious can assist the mental shifts necessary to move from disagreement to collective alignment. It is of great importance to go through a process where everyone in the group feels heard and whole.

Whatever spiritual practice used, the idea is to get the entire group in a "feeling" that an agreement is possible. A "feeling" that allows each person to declare a "willingness" to engage toward a collective solution. When an entire group can agree on a high level of willingness to agree, providence moves, evolution of thought can take place and fresh ideas have a path for expression. It will be the "feeling of agreement" that can be the catalyst for opening of the way toward listening and hearing, even before the issues are discussed. This is the vibration of synergy that emanates from unity.

Six ideas for Increasing the Availability of Funds

I remind you, the reader, that this was *our* experience presented through the lens of my personal perspective. Again, I say use the banquet approach. If none of this adds a blessing to your ministry, let it be a discussion starter for boards to work through the kinds of issues that arise in the course of ministry growth and board service.

One: Tithing as a Ministry

Whether it is due to challenging financial times, or uncertainty felt in the ministry if there is a delay in "cash flow," it is a great time for the board to assess its tithing practices. Yes, just as in the case of individuals and families, during challenging times, the board may allow the ministry to become lax in tithing. It may happen also that tithing becomes a burden rather than the joy of giving back to God's work—which has the same effect as not tithing. "Each of you should give what you have decided in your heart to give, not reluctantly or under compulsion, for God loves a cheerful giver," --2 Corinthians 9:7 (NIV).

In truth we never want to give in to the appearance of lack or fall into believing and thinking we do not have enough. We know all the spiritual principles that tell us God is our Source. We practice, teach and preach biblical positions on tithing. From the book of Malachi to what Jesus tells us in the gospel of Luke, we may choose tithing as a key strategy in building a prosperity consciousness in ministry affairs.

> "I the LORD do not change. So you, the descendants of Jacob, are not destroyed. Ever since the time of your ancestors you have turned away from my decrees and have not kept them. Return to me, and I will return to you," says the LORD Almighty. "But you ask, 'How are we to return?'
>
> "Will a mere mortal rob God? Yet you rob me.
>
> "But you ask, 'How are we robbing you?'
> "In tithes and offerings. You are under a curse—your whole nation—because you are robbing me. Bring the whole tithe into the storehouse, that there may be food in my house. Test me in this," says the LORD Almighty, "and see if I will not throw open the floodgates of heaven and pour out so much blessing that there will not be room enough to store it," (Malachi 3:6-10 NIV).

Jesus did not talk specifically about tithing but did give a great lesson on the law of giving and receiving:

> "Do not judge, and you will not be judged; do not condemn, and you will not be condemned. Forgive, and you will be forgiven; give, and it will be given to you. A good measure, pressed down, shaken together, running over, will be put into your lap; for the measure you give will be the measure you get back," (Luke 6:37-38 NRSV).

In our ministry there was a time when we fell short in our tithing. We decided to acknowledge, correct, forgive and move forward—get back on the track to tithing as soon as we were able. Tithing as a spiritual principle is another good point around which the board could benefit by being of one accord.

Two: Decrease Expenses

This was my least favorite to discuss in our ministry. However, we did as we felt it needed to be done. Let me assume that the budget for your ministry is not padded with a lot of unnecessary items. Generally, this is the case with a non-profit organization. We are conscious of expenditures and seek to meet a prayerfully crafted budget. Additionally, I also assume that as part of standard operating procedures your ministry has a system of checks and balances to assure accurate reporting and recording of income as well as expenses. All this being said, there may still be times when a reduction in expenses is necessary.

The first time we had an audit of our finances, we were concerned about spending money for the cost of the audit. Nevertheless, we discovered that the audit was well worth the fee. It revealed areas where greater efficiency in our operations would actually save money. Most likely a ministry will not need an audit every year. An exception to this will be determined by the ministry size, goals and engagement in specific projects that may require audited financials. For several years we applied for and received grants that were Federally, State and locally funded and audited financials were required.

Some ministries have a budget team, finance team or as we referred to ours "Financial Stability Team" to review the budget and church finances to make recommendations. This way the board has the benefit of having the finances reviewed through eyes of those who can give an objective financial opinion.

It is important to approach decreasing expenses as a positive rather than a negative. I have grown to embrace a budget review as an opportunity to increase our efficiency and improve ongoing good stewardship. Surely, we shall balance wisdom and compassion in budgetary reductions. Our spirituality calls us to remember that people's lives may be affected by any cut-backs we might make.

Three: Open to New Streams of Income

This section should probably go without saying, but I have such a great appreciation for the discussion that I wanted to include it. We certainly do all we can as ministry leaders to assure that we have funds available to operate and grow the ministry. However, there are simply times we could certainly appreciate financial support beyond the funds that come from members. "But thou shalt remember the LORD thy God: for it is he that giveth thee power to get wealth, that he may establish his covenant which he sware unto thy fathers, as it is this day," (Deuteronomy 8:18).

We discovered that when we opened our consciousness through prayer to streams of income, new channels became available to us. Of course, we were always open, but when we set in prayer the idea that *income flows to us from every direction and through unlimited avenues, expected and unexpected*, we literally had opportunities show up on our doorstep.

Some of what we have experienced is renting space to another church, renting space to other groups, rentals for weddings, banquets and parties.[6] We have rented space to the county where our facility was used as an election polling place. We joined with the promoters of a major musical group and presented a VIP opening reception for their concert. The point is we did not go out to enlist these channels. They were initiated by someone literally knocking on the door of our center once we declared that we were open to additional channels of income.

Four: Capital Campaigns

One thing I know for sure: Seek first the kingdom of God before embarking on a capital campaign.

Generally, a capital campaign is implemented to raise funds for projects requiring larger sums of money. The board will want to gain as much knowledge as possible before making the decision to launch such a program. It is important to weigh options of using a professional fundraising organization or using resources available within the congregation. Either way a capital campaign will work best when great

---

6 Decide on a policy regarding alcohol consumption on the premises.

effort is put into the preparation phase that includes prayer and logistics followed by the implementation of a well-timed effort.

Our first capital campaign was done as a bond program which of course is a professional fundraising project. So, we learned a lot from the professionals and then decided to do subsequent capital campaign programs on our own and with reasonable success.

Five: Borrowing Funds
Here I'm referring to raising larger sums of funds such as amounts necessary for a mortgage or a refinance situation. This is an area where many ministries find it challenging to acquire financing. Unless your ministry operates at a high level of revenue over expenses, has large sums of cash available, or has accumulated the kind of assets that look good on a balance sheet, you may discover that banks have some reluctance to loaning greater sums of money to churches and religious organizations. As I was told by a banker at one of the five banks that rejected our application for a six hundred-thousand-dollar mortgage loan, "Nobody wants to be the one who forecloses on a church or house of God." and, "since non-profit religious organizations rely on charitable donations to keep the doors open, there is too great a risk in uncertain economic times." Their thinking is that if funds get tight for families, through economic ups and downs, they cut back on charitable giving first—putting the church's offerings at risk.

With their reluctance, banks generally perceive large church loans so risky that they come up with strategies to "over" secure the loan. Several of the banks we applied to asked that the full board and spiritual leader personally guarantee the loan in addition to the security of the property. We decided to pray for other options that did indeed manifest. "And God is able to make all grace abound toward you; that ye, always having all sufficiency in all things, may abound to every good work," (2 Corinthians 9:8).

The subject of debt is where we are challenged to balance our spiritual laws and material realm existence into a unified board position. The banks don't particularly want to loan money to churches and we don't want to be in a position where we need to borrow money from them. No ministry wants to carry large sums of debt on its balance sheet for obvious financial reasons and also because of the metaphysical perspective regarding debt. In his book *Prosperity*, Charles Fillmore says,

> Debt is a contradiction of the universal equilibrium, and there is no such thing as a lack of equilibrium in all the universe. Therefore, in Spirit and in Truth there is no debt. However, men hold on to a thought of debt, and this thought is responsible for a great deal of sorrow and hardship. The true disciple realizes his supply in the consciousness of omnipresent, universally possessed abundance. Spirit substance is impartial and owned in common, and no thought of debt can enter into it.
>
> Debt is a thought of lack with absence at both ends; the creditor thinks he lacks what is owed him and the debtor thinks he lacks what is necessary to pay it, else he would discharge the obligation rather than continue it.

Therein is an agreement issue for which the board will want to discuss before signing on the bottom line of a debt instrument. In Spirit and in truth there is no such thing as debt. Yet, in the material realm of earthly finance, debt is the major avenue we have culturally accepted as our solution to getting what we want. The moment we accept that debt is a reality for our ministry we open the door and agree that debt does indeed exist as a form of lack in our consciousness. Now I am not at all suggesting that we not take out a mortgage to purchase or build the physical structure of our new spiritual home. But I think it is important to have a thorough discussion of debt at the boardroom table before opening that door. Again, I say reaching agreement before the decision can help to avert misunderstandings and disharmony later on. Not to be concerned, however, for in the same book, Charles Fillmore tells us that if we do have debt, he says, "God will pay your debts," and he proceeds to tell us how.

Creative Borrowing or Invest Where You Pray

Here I discuss two programs that worked well for our ministry when we desired to increase available funds while addressing the idea of debt at the same time.

I. Church Bonds

A bond program is a particular type of capital campaign that has the added feature of investment opportunity for the ministry members. We were introduced to the opportunity of offering church bonds to our congregation to raise the funds for the purchase of our property. It was a grueling process to meet the financial due diligence in order to meet all the legal and governmental regulations and requirements that would demonstrate our credit worthiness. That process alone helped our board to have a much better grasp on our ministry's financial position. It was its own educational process.

Those who purchased the bonds became the mortgage holders of the church. The members of the spiritual community own a stake in the property and building.

Just as investors put their dollars in major corporations and risk repayment according to the success or failure of the corporation, so it is when investing in church bonds. Except that members of the ministry have a direct influence over the ministry's ability to repay the investors. By and through active involvement and participation in the ministry, members who are also investors have the added opportunity to assure that the ministry succeeds.

A bond program as an investment in your spiritual community is indeed a great avenue for providing funds to keep it growing forward and thereby assure that God's work will continue and be a blessing to present and future members.

From the standpoint of ministry leadership, if a mortgage is needed a bond program can make available an opportunity for members to invest where:

- they pray,
- receive their spiritual nourishment,
- volunteer their time and talent,
- give of their tithes and offerings.

All this while receiving a competitive interest rate on funds invested makes this type of opportunity a prosperity program like no other.

A Solution for the Debt Dilemma

There is another angle on why a bond program can be a good mortgage finance vehicle for a spiritual community. A bond program addresses our previous discussion regarding debt in a unique way. The debt being created by issuing bonds to purchase or build a physical spiritual home using member generated funds, is likened to the ministry raising money from itself, for itself. The investors will be paying themselves back with interest while enjoying the benefits for which the loan was made—a physical structure, a place for the work of God. Additionally, if the members are also tithers, they will prosper by way of the interest paid on their investment and thereby experience an increase on what they have to tithe on—good for them and good for the ministry. "Let no debt remain outstanding, except the continuing debt to love one another, for whoever loves others has fulfilled the law," (Romans 13:8 NIV).

Circulating funds within the ministry allows members to become the solution to the ministry's financial opportunity. The idea of debt is addressed when creditor and debtor are one in the same—no debt in Spirit and in truth. When mortgagor and mortgagee are one in the same, a unique position is created that can influence and assure a good outcome for the ministry and the investor. I like to think of it as an "invest where you pray prosperity program."

In our ministry when we raised funds through our bond program, the board designated a tithe from the ministry to invest in four bonds which we granted to four children as a college set aside. We made it a writing contest for the youth program and made a big deal out of the importance of college for our children. We saw this as the church planting seeds of growth in our future by way of investing in our children—Priceless!

II.   <u>Investment Club</u>

With all of the above stated benefits described for the bond program, an investment club made up of members was formed. Several years after purchasing the property we found ourselves in need of funds when we met with "trouble" over an issue of payroll taxes with the IRS.[7] Members of the ministry formed a legally registered investment club.[8] A legally drawn and executed promissory note and second mortgage was made with the ministry. An attractive interest rate made it a good investment for the members, and the ministry was able to meet an immediate demand for funds. Again, when debtor and creditor is the same, from the metaphysical perspective no debt is created.

Six: Financial Stimulus Activities

I am not promoting any of the activities listed in this section. This list is presented simply to suggest that there are many, many things that can be done when a ministry has more of an immediate financial need or the desire to fund a project that is outside or beyond the funds made available in the budget.

We found that there were times when we needed or wanted funds for a specific effort and decided to create an income opportunity to raise the funds desired. Following is a general list of things we have done over a nineteen-year period. Perhaps your ministry has done some of these and could add many more to this list. As I am not recommending any of these, consider them as conversation starters for fundraising ideas that you may develop for use in your ministry. Additionally, I respect those who believe that fundraising should not have a place in ministry and therefore, I respectfully say, feel free to skip the balance of this section if you are in that belief.

We did many of these things (not all) under the umbrella of our "fundraising team." However, there was a lot of focus on "fun" and that made all the difference in the overall success and value of these events. We used the desire to raise funds as an opportunity to build community

---

7 Note regarding payroll taxes: PAY THEM! Pay them on time and in full! Enough Said!

8 The Investment Club is not an entity of the church. Neither the minister, nor the board of trustees has any authority over the Investment Club except to the extent that they are members of the club along with every other investor. The Investment Club has its own set of by-laws, policies and procedures and board of trustees.

and as bonding experiences for the congregation. The amount of funds raised for each of these activities (after expenses) ranged from $2,500 to $30,000. Obviously, the size of a ministry, the enthusiasm generated and the strategy by which the project is implemented will help craft the amount of funds generated. We found that prayer, great planning and commitment from the full board of trustees had a great impact on our success with any one event. "Sow your seed in the morning, and at evening let your hands not be idle, for you do not know which will succeed, whether this or that, or whether both will do equally well," (Ecclesiastes 11:6 NIV).

- Themed banquet

- Automobile raffle

- Silent and live auctions

- Jazz for Jesus Concert

- VIP Musical Concert

- Sports tournaments

- Congregational Authored Book

- Youth Summer Camp (children are not fundraisers but grants for children's programs are available)

- Tea Party

- Donor Luncheon

- Dine and Dash

- Dance Contest

- Avocado Festival (This works best if you have an avocado grove. But perhaps you have something else unique to your ministry.)

- Travel Programs

- Spiritual programs that invite unexpected income offerings

The appearance of financial challenges can be overcome as Spirit works through "called" leaders who endeavor to keep the ministry abiding by spiritual laws that support increase and multiply substance.

Affirmation for Spiritual Key #6:

We claim the rewards embedded in the power of agreement as we make sound decisions with wisdom, compassion and unity.

6th Spiritual Key: AGREEMENT

1. Approach all financial related matters by using our spiritual practices to invoke the power of agreement.

2. With one accord strive to operate ministry affairs within the bounds of divine laws that govern giving and receiving.

3. In decision making processes, we synchronize our group energy to harness the synergy that allows harmony and agreement to unfold.

  • In his book *Prosperity*, Charles Fillmore says, "Watch your thoughts when you are handling money, because money is attached to you through your mind to the one source of all substance." For board members, this should be true on a personal level as well as in handling money on behalf of the ministry. Fillmore's statement includes those times when counting the ministry funds, writing or signing checks, when viewing the ministry financial statements and in discussions around the boardroom table. As a leader in the ministry, the consciousness of the trustees matters greatly.

  • If it is determined that expenses must be reduced, do it with wisdom and compassion. Factor in the decision the ministry's mission, vision and values statements.

  • If you reach a state where the ministry has fallen away from tithing for a time. This is not cause to claim guilt or cast blame. Do not let a tithe become a debt. Total the amount that would have been paid as a tithe, say a prayer of forgiveness over those tithes and send divine love, appreciation and gratitude to the places where the tithes would have gone. Get back on the path to tithing as soon as possible—not out of obligation but for the joy of giving.

  • Pray together before a major financial decision. If possible, take the time you need – Spirit operates on divine timing. Most decisions allow for time to do our due diligence. If time is of the essence and there is no time to stop and assess, this could be a signal that some greater lesson is to be revealed. I like the seven-day prayer technique. According to the allegory in Genesis, God took seven days to create the earth and after that cycle of completion *behold it was very good.* So, if possible take at least seven consistent days to prayerfully seek the guidance you desire. If the whole board agrees to pray daily over an issue and come back on the eighth day to make the decision, this may offer some level of comfort rather than rushing into a decision.

• Where financial issues are concerned, prayerfully select and consult with professionals who can offer legal, accounting and financial advice. As a board of a spiritual organization we must still abide by the "laws of the land."

• Have in place sound checks and balances for the flow of money in and out of the ministry. Ideally those sound financial practices will "protect" those who have access to money and finance records from ever being in a situation where they could be accused of some inappropriate maneuver. Jesus prayed in this way "leave us not in temptation." Leave no member of the board open to the possibility of their integrity or honesty being questioned regarding the funds of the ministry.

Discussion Starters for Board Bonding - Agreement

1. Discuss your understanding of the spiritual message behind the experience of being in financial "need."

2. To what degree do the individual giving habits of board members contribute to the overall financial outlook for the church/center?

3. Craft a generalized approach the board could use toward working through a financial challenge.

4. As you share of your financial treasure, to what degree can you say that you do so with joy, gratitude and thanksgiving? How do you demonstrate this?

5. Recall a time when the board had 100% agreement on an issue facing the board for resolution? How did it feel to be of One Accord? Did you harness the feeling of synergy among members of the board?

If the leadership of the ministry has a commitment to operate with "one accord" the tone for harmony will be felt at the boardroom table and its vibration of peace will radiate throughout the spiritual community.

Chapter Seven

Leave a Gift at the Table

LEGACY

"A new commandment I give to you, that you love one another; as I
have loved you, that you also love one another."

--John 13:34 (NKJV)

Jesus left the gift of love for all of us through his teachings, and the
path of enlightenment he paved for us to follow. The above referenced
scripture points out that Jesus did not just tell his disciples to love, he set
the example first.

Hope for the Future

When Jesus was preparing for his final exit from the disciples he left
with them an intention that the work would continue. "He said to him
the third time, "Simon, *son* of Jonah, do you love Me?" Peter was grieved
because He said to him the third time, "Do you love Me?" And he said to
Him, "Lord, You know all things; You know that I love You." Jesus said to
him, "Feed My sheep," (John 21:17-18 NKJV).

When it is time for a change at the boardroom table, whether board
member or spiritual leader, all will have the same sentiment that Jesus
had leaving the disciples, feed my sheep. In other words, keep serving
humankind by continuing to feed the malnourished souls that

hunger to know God, Truth, the abundant life and their own divine perfection. We will want those who remain to continue to support and guide others on their spiritual path. As we leave the table, let us affirm wholeness, health, peace and prosperity for all who enjoy the benefits of the ministry.

To have a seat at the boardroom table is a great opportunity to set policies, goals and dreams that affect the lives of present members. But leadership is at its best when we honor our present and remain mindful that choices and decisions made currently will have consequences for future members, boards and spiritual leaders that will come long after our tenure. *"In our every deliberation, we must consider the impact of our decisions on the next seven generations."*[9]

Just a few months after we purchased our five-acre avocado grove, we were approached by a developer who wanted to purchase the property for one million dollars above what we paid for it. Well, we knew that we would not find a piece of land as beautiful, in the same area, so we declined their offer. Several months later the developer came again asking if we would divide the land and sell them half of our five acres for one million dollars above what we paid.

At first, we thought it to be the answer to our prayer and we began negotiations with them. But when we did our prayer of discernment, what came to the full board was that someday maybe ten, twenty who knows thirty years down the road, the board at that future time would be grateful to have five acres to fulfill the mission of the ministry for their time. There would be room and space to grow into a larger vision. We decided to keep and care for the land they would inherit and prayed that future generations would be good stewards over the property we made "sacrifices" to keep.

When we shared with the congregation our guidance not to continue negotiations with the developers, our confirmation came with a unanimous agreement from the members.

9 Iroquois Maxim (circa 1700-1800)

Dream a Big Dream

A few years after we purchased our property we planned a big anniversary celebration. In preparation for the big event, I began looking through some of the history records of the ministry searching for something we could use to honor our journey. I discovered a twenty-five-year-old newspaper article in the Miami Times. The minister of our church at that time, Rev. Loren Flickinger was quoted in an interview as saying, "We are looking for about five acres of land to build our church on." I was nearly in tears; it was a confirmation that we were on the right path. Although it was twenty-five years in the making, and some twenty years after his tenure Flickinger's dream had come to pass. I was able to contact Rev. Flickinger and invite him to come to our anniversary celebration that year on the five-acre piece of land he had dreamed of in the early days. He was experiencing ill health at the time, but his wife made sure that they visited on the Anniversary Sunday. He was in a wheelchair and could barely speak but was able to see and enjoy the realization and manifestation of his earlier words. Rev. Flickinger made his transition not long after.

The practices set in motion by the board of trustees and the spiritual leader, shall become a guide and the inheritance for those who serve in the future. The great value of your service and leadership may not be fully evident in your tenure. Many of the programs, policies and decisions made at the boardroom table will have long range consequences for future boards, spiritual leaders and members of the ministry.

As leaders we make choices for the current time but let us not underestimate the great value our decisions, choices and dreams can have on the future of the ministry. Your service will become a matter of record and influence the unfolding history of the faith community you have given your precious time, talent and treasure.

Let it be known that harmony at the boardroom table is a commitment on the leadership level of the ministry. The current board has the potential to set in place a relationship model that will allow time on the board to be one of personal and spiritual growth. In addition, the quality of your experience will bless your successors and the generations who will benefit from your legacy. Let that legacy, whether board member or spiritual leader, be one that honors God, practices the teachings of Jesus Christ, celebrates life, joyfully follows a positive path that is of high quality, and leaves a big dream that will, in time, show itself as a divine blessing for the ministry.

A Plan for Changing Seasons

One of the scriptures I have found to be helpful over my years in ministry is Ecclesiastes 3:1 (NRSV), "For everything there is a season, and a time for every matter under heaven."

It reminds me that there is an order to all things; a divine order that grows, evolves and changes in cycles and moves according to God's perfectly orchestrated rhythm. Change is not always easy to face in ministry, so it helps to acknowledge that it will indeed happen and do the best we can to prepare for it and grow through it.

While the past cannot be changed, if I granted myself just one moment to flirt with the idea that it could, it would have been concerning being better prepared for change—like the impending change that was revealed to Pharaoh in a dream and interpreted by Joseph.

> "There will come seven years of great plenty throughout all the land of Egypt. After them there will arise seven years of famine, and all the plenty will be forgotten in the land of Egypt; the famine will consume the land. The plenty will no longer be known in the land because of the famine that will follow, for it will be very grievous. And the doubling of Pharaoh's dream means that the thing is fixed by God, and God will shortly bring it about," (Genesis 41:29-32 NRSV).

The seven years of plenty followed by seven years of famine speaks to cycles of growth and evolution. Within a cycle there will appear to be a time of withholding, a pause in forward movement, a seeming deficiency in resources, a time of under-performance from the previous stage. But the stage of seeming inactivity is necessary to give the following stage added energy to once again grow forward and flourish. If we notice nature's illustration of change from season to season, we can grasp the divine order of change, and gain an appreciation of the cycles we face in our own lives and within the evolution of our ministry. The winter season holds the promise of spring when all things are made new.

We experienced several (more than seven) years of plenty only to find ourselves in the midst of a decrease in income resulting from economic shifts beyond our ministry. With very little in reserve when things got rough, decisions were made that took years to work through the consequences of those decisions.

Boards of trustees, acting with the spiritual leader have the charge to plan for the future health, growth and prosperity of the ministry and that means taking into consideration the rhythm of change and the divine order of cycles.

The congregation will change over time. The board members serving at the table will change over time. The spiritual leader will change over time. The economy will change over time. Societal shifts will change over time. Ways and methods of doing ministry will change over time. That's a lot of change!

It is worth it to have a strategic plan that calculates the ministry's growth chart going forward. That strategic plan will allow attention toward expected and unexpected effects of cyclical, economic and cultural shifts. In other words, we monitor where we are, and build in sound prayerful strategic practices to embrace inevitable change as best we can predict by trends and forecasts. Beyond doing our preparation work, we trust that we shall be divinely guided—no matter the changes ahead.

Tell the Stories that Reveal God's Presence

When it is our time to leave the boardroom table, tell the stories that lift the ministry and acknowledge God's presence at work. We may have had some challenging experiences during our tenure on the board. However, in the principles we live and teach we know that more can be done for the ministry with words that build up than from words that tear down.

Promote the good. Focus on the positive. Tell stories that inspire the minds and hearts of members to know and feel God's presence in the ministry they love.

Following are two stories I love to tell. Both are of a time when our board had to work through disagreement and arrived at positive outcomes from our willingness to be of one accord. After we purchased the property, we had some difficult decisions to make and the board seemed to be divided on a few of them.

Story Number One

We inherited a beautiful in-ground, heated, screened-in swimming pool on the property we purchased. What to do with the swimming pool was a discussion on every board agenda for over a year. Some wanted to keep the pool, others did not. Because we wanted to reach a "harmonious" decision we delayed, discussed, delayed, discussed until finally the liability laid out to us by our insurance company helped us to reach a difficult but unanimous decision. So, we had a big "fill in the swimming pool celebration." Congregants gathered as the contractors were filling in the pool and each person present placed an angel prayer card between or on top of the rocks before the top cement was poured as the new patio floor. Afterwards we placed a four-foot plaque erected at the entrance of the patio telling the story of the angel cards located just below the concrete floor. Upon entering each person is encouraged to say a prayer knowing their prayer will have the attention and support of Angels. A difficult decision was turned into a positive blessing. "For he shall give his angels charge over thee, to keep thee in all thy ways. They shall bear thee up in their hands, lest thou dash thy foot against a stone," (Psalm 91:11-12).

Story Number Two

Just after the swimming pool decision, we had another big opportunity to arrive at a place of one accord. We had about 250 avocado trees in the front of the property and 250 avocado trees in the back portion of the land divided by two buildings sitting directly in the center of property. We needed to decide which trees should be eliminated so that we could build and have space for parking. The board was divided. We had congregants who did not want to be part of a massive tree cutting effort. We even had a split decision between architect and builder. There seemed to be no easy solution. So, we continued to pray for guidance with a commitment to maintain harmony by way of a unanimous decision. We wanted to feel the connectedness in decision making we knew was possible based on past experiences.

Months and months went by. Now this was in 2005 and when June 1st came around, we did what we had done for many years—say a special prayer straight through the end of hurricane season which ends December 1st. As a congregation we affirm for the entire six-month period: "Divine love expresses through the weather patterns yielding divine order and operating under divine perfection."

August of 2005, Hurricane Katrina wiped out about fifty trees in the front. When the board convened of course we were a bit overcome to see the destruction of our beautiful trees. However, some felt this was Spirit's message that the front trees should be those to go and where we should build. However, the fifty trees that were uprooted were concentrated in one area and made for a nice clearing at the entrance of the property. This left some members of the board still unsure as to if clearing the rest of trees from the front was Spirit's intended message.

Two months later hurricane Wilma uprooted an additional one hundred twenty-five trees—from the front. Because of the age of the trees, we were advised not to try and replant them. No harm was done to the back portion of the avocado grove nor was either of the buildings damaged in any way. The guidance was clear and there was no doubt.

So the prayer we had been praying for guidance on where to build was answered by our affirmation for hurricane season. The answer to our prayer came as *Divine love expresses through the weather patterns yielding divine order and operating under divine perfection.*

By the power of divine love, the earth gave up one hundred and seventy-five avocado trees in a visual that looked like a carefully sculpted design of nature's response to the board's dilemma. The gratitude that we felt for not having to put a saw blade on one single tree but rather stand down and allow the wind of Spirit to lift each tree from the earth and gently lay them aside one by one felt like a moment of grace.

We had our answer, and everyone was clear it had been a Spirit guided message.

Sharing of our stories can be a blessing of inspiration as every member wants to know that the power of God is at work through the leadership of their ministry. The stories we tell as we exit our term on the board will also be a testament to the quality of our experience at the boardroom table—and thereby a reflection of our own consciousness.

Stay Centered on What Guided You to Serve

Once we get immersed in the affairs of the ministry, it is easy to forget *why* we give of our time, talent and treasure for the opportunity to sit at the boardroom table.

During financially challenged times we may allow the finances to become all-consuming. Or, there may be times when the actions or inactions of members of the ministry become the focus and excuse for why things didn't go as we had hoped. There may even be times when we find ourselves focused on personalities (for or against) of those around the table rather than the issues on the table. Yes, if we are not vigilant, we can allow distractions of our energy away from the mission, vision and values.

Many years ago, we had a board member who had difficulty with a particular issue facing the board and he strongly disagreed. As time when on, I noticed that this board member befriended another member of the board and as their relationship grew I noticed the two of them taking the same stance on several issues as they came up for discussion. Because we maintain peace and harmony on the board, several times issues were delayed due to the two members who stood together in disagreement. Finally, the situation ended with the first board member resigning. The second board member came to me and when she asked if she could talk with me and closed my door, I was prepared for her resignation as well. However, she sat and immediately tears began to flow, "I had forgotten why I am on the board. I love our ministry, I love the people here, I believe in God and I love truth—that's why I'm here." She went on to complete her term on the board.

In my own journey of ministry, I have discovered that the times I struggled with issues in our church where those times I found myself immersed in ministry affairs to the point of setting aside my focus from my "call" to ministry. I have learned the importance of keeping my purpose for serving fresh in my heart and mind. I find that board members work well through the challenges we face when they too remember why they serve.

Each member who sits at the boardroom table has the privilege to develop his or her own faculties of mind in their personal life. However, if prominent, three attitudes of mind can particularly benefit the work and affairs we address in the exercise of board service. By Jesus' example we see that he worked well with all the disciples. Yet, there were three who went with him most often: the disciples that represent faith, love and wisdom.

We sit at the table as an act of our faith in God, for the purpose of giving and sharing love, with the prayer that our decisions will be wise for the overall good of the ministry.

If we hold ourselves to a standard of faith, love and wisdom while keeping fresh before us, our "call" to serve, we shall continue to give the best of who we are during and long after our tenure is complete.

On occasion we should ask ourselves, *Why am I here?* If we stay connected to our purpose for saying "Yes" to board service, "Yes" to Spirit's call, we will find the faith, love and wisdom to act along with other members of the board with one accord.

Own the Honor of Having Had a Seat at the Table

From days of old, to be invited to sit at the table of leadership was itself a show of respect and considered to be an act of privilege.

At the table of his last Passover meal Jesus made an impassioned speech to the disciples seated with him.

> "Out in the world the master sits at the table and is served by his servants. But not here! For I am your servant. Nevertheless, because you have stood true to me in these terrible days, and because my Father has granted me a Kingdom, I, here and now, grant you the right to eat and drink at my table in that Kingdom; and you will sit on thrones judging the twelve tribes of Israel," (Luke 22:27-30 TLB).

Great responsibility rests upon the shoulders of those who sit at the table of leadership. At that table, respect and appreciation has a chance to grow through the trials, issues and experiences shared. The true gift of service is to own it as a blessing to give of time, talent and treasure to further the work of the Christ presence at the table in the ministry and in the world. We gain the full gift of this opportunity when we own the opportunity to give generously from a heart of compassion, the joy of service, and the wisdom that flows through us in prayerful, discerning, thoughtful words and actions.

Yes, there may have been times in our board service when we fell short of our mark of perfection. However, the more important issue will be, did we give up or did we continue to strive for greater, better, or the improved version of ourselves?

And when it is time to step away from your seat at the table, pass the baton with no regrets. Position yourself to look back at Spirit's call, and know you gave your best. Yes, this is a worthy legacy.

File it away in your mind that during your tenure you made a difference. Let there be peace in your heart knowing that during your term on the board of trustees you participated on a Spirit guided team with one accord—one with Spirit, and one with those with whom you served.

Know that at the table of leadership you contributed your best in a spiritual partnership that impacted the lives of others greatly. As you served God with a heart of compassion, the vision of your ministry is a little closer to fulfillment. Is there any greater joy in spiritual work than to be used by Spirit toward a great mission, and a life-transforming cause?

Affirmation for Spiritual Key #7:

We thrive in a rich unfolding legacy of faith, wisdom and compassion whose gifts reach far into time and space of many tomorrows.

7ᵗʰ Spiritual Key: LEGACY

1. As you step away from board service, honor the spiritual partnership shared with a divinely appointed team, as one of life's great gifts.

2. Leave a legacy that will be richly endowed with your generous contributions of time, talent and treasure toward a transforming mission, vision and values of a great cause.

3. Your service has prepared you to fully embrace that which Spirit has in store for you. Enjoy your next assignment!

- Legacy matters. Be vigilant over the idea that you will leave something behind when your tenure is complete, by way of attitude, consciousness, policies, procedures or material manifestations. Your legacy will make a difference in the affairs of the ministry—some things in minor ways and others in major ways.

- When making decisions on behalf of the ministry take the time to weigh the long-range consequences with the immediate effects.

- Once a board member always a board member. Continue to hold the leadership team in prayer, even after you leave. Keep in mind how much you would have appreciated such support when you were actively serving.

- After leaving board service, continue to make yourself available to the current board if asked for counsel or sought out in an advisory capacity. Your willingness to support a project can be a way of continuing to make a difference.

-
- Find ways and opportunities to express gratitude for board members and spiritual leaders during their tenure and as they leave their seat on the board. We implemented an annual *Present and Past Board Member Luncheon.* During

this event current board members honor past board members with lunch and updates on the current goals, and future plans for the ministry; spouses and partners were invited to this luncheon as well.

- Let gratitude be the rule of thumb when there is a change in leadership whether board members or spiritual leaders. We can never show too much love and appreciation for those who serve our ministry with their love and commitment. "And we know that all things work together for good to them that love God, to them who are the called according to his purpose," (Romans 8:28).

Discussion Starters for Board Bonding – Legacy

1. Does the board have shared dreams, goals or a desired legacy project that drives decisions and choices?

2. Does the board know of the minister/spiritual leader's dreams for the church/center?

3. What would you say the founding board left as their legacy for the current board?

4. What will be your "gift" when it is your time to leave the board?

5. Tell a story regarding your service on the board that has personal meaning and value to you, the kind of story that you will carry with you as a good memory.

Now the God of endurance and of encouragement give to you to be like-minded one toward another, according to Christ Jesus; that ye may with one accord, with one mouth, glorify the God and Father of our Lord Jesus Christ.

Romans 15:5-6 (DARBY)

APPENDIX I

Scripturally-based Code of Conduct

We, members of the Board of Trustee of _____, bound together by the mission, vision and values of this spiritual community, agree to serve with One Accord and in harmony, that we may lead a life worthy of the calling to which we have been called, with all humility and gentleness, with patience, bearing with one another in love, making every effort to maintain the unity of the Spirit in the bond of peace. There is one body and one Spirit, just as you were called to the one hope of your calling, one Lord, one faith, one baptism, one God and Father of all, who is above all and through all and in all.

(Adapted from Ephesians 4:1-6 using the NRSV)

To adopt, print out a copy and each member should sign it. Post it where it shall be a reminder of the commitment.

APPENDIX II

Ministry Prayer and Blessing
Fill in the blanks with the name of your ministry and affirm together as a full board.

_____ now flourishes under the banner of divine love.

The wisdom of Spirit now prevails in and through the affairs of this ministry as divine guidance, and divine order.

All those in a leadership capacity on behalf of this ministry are hereby consciously governed under divine law and therefore in unity with the Christ Mind.

This ministry now thrives in the all-sufficiency of God's holy presence manifesting unlimited bounty from God's rich storehouse of abundance.

Every friend, visitor and member will enter our doors and feel the presence of peace, kindness and compassion.

Let us know together that there is only one presence and one power being Itself in and through _____ now.

We radiate a consciousness of faith, in all that we undertake.

With One Accord, unified by the grace of God, we join with communities of faith around the world upholding a sacred vision of peace and prosperity for all.

Amen!

About the Author

Charline E. Manuel is founder and chief executive of One Accord Strategies, Inc. a Maryland-based, not-for-profit company. Charline works with nonprofit organizations strengthening their board leadership capacity. She conducts workshops, seminars and retreats empowering boards with education and training through programs on topics of Inclusive Leadership, Board Enrichment, Effective Governance and Compassionate leadership, and her signature board program, *The Power of One Accord*, using her book by the same title.

Having served on several nonprofit boards for over twenty-five years, Charline developed a passion for helping boards raise their effectiveness through building harmonious and high functioning relationships at the boardroom table. She has traveled extensively to work with boards of organizations whose fulfilled missions can lead to a more peaceful world.

An ordained a Unity minister, she served as a senior minister and pastor for twenty-two years in Miami, Florida. She has served as adjunct faculty for the Unity Urban seminary, teaching subjects on Ethics for Spiritual leaders, Working with Church Boards and Homiletics. Her international travels have led her to organize mission trips for clean water in West Africa, building a school in Haiti, peace immersion at the United Nations mandated University for Peace in Costa Rica, and participation in several of the Parliament of the World's Religions conventions.

Charline is author of five books including best sellers, *Pray Up Your Life* and children's book *Do Puppies Pray*. She makes her home in Columbia, Maryland.

For more information about Charline and her work, please visit *oneaccordstrategies.org*.